ILLINOIS CENTRAL COLLEGE
JX1974.7.A672
STACKS
Arms control /

A12900 365733

THE REFERENCE SHELF

WITHDRAWN

WITHDRAWN

ARMS CONTROL

edited by WILLIAM P. LINEBERRY

THE REFERENCE SHELF
Volume 51 Number 6

THE H. W. WILSON COMPANY
New York 1979

I. C. C. LIBRARY 65431

THE REFERENCE SHELF

The books in this series contain reprints of articles, excerpts from books, and addresses on current issues and social trends in the United States and other countries. There are six separately bound numbers in each volume, all of which are generally published in the same calendar year. One number is a collection of recent speeches; each of the others is devoted to a single subject and gives background information and discussion from various points of view, concluding with a comprehensive bibliography. Books in the series may be purchased individually or on subscription.

Library of Congress Cataloging in Publication Data
Main entry under title:

Arms control

   (The Reference shelf; v. 51, no. 6)
   Bibliography: p.
   1. Atomic weapons and disarmament—Addresses, essays, lectures. 2. Arms control—Addresses, essays, lectures. I. Lineberry, William P.
II. Series: Reference shelf; v. 51, no. 6.
JX1974.7.A672   327'.174   79-24150
ISBN 0-8242-0636-3

Copyright © 1979 by The H. W. Wilson Company. All rights reserved. No part of this work may be reproduced or copied in any form or by any means, including but not restricted to graphic, electronic, and mechanical—for example, photocopying, recording, taping, or information and retrieval systems—without the express written permission of the publisher, except that a reviewer may quote and a magazine or newspaper may print brief passages as part of a review written specifically for inclusion in that magazine or newspaper.

PRINTED IN THE UNITED STATES OF AMERICA

PREFACE

When the United Nations General Assembly met in special session in 1978 to discuss the prospects for world disarmament, one delegate wanted to know why it was, when speaker after speaker from nation after nation spoke for disarmament so strongly and so eloquently, that no real progress in the matter seemed to be made. In a sense, the delegate's question is the real subject of this compilation. Most of the articles that follow focus on one or another aspect of arms control—particularly the SALT II agreement—but throughout is an underlying tone of despair that any treaty can significantly reduce the steady buildup of worldwide weaponry.

Arms—by which we mean nuclear weapons—are controlled through international agreements such as SALT and the nuclear Non-Proliferation Treaty (NPT), but these pacts can prevent neither modern science and technology from roaming over vast and unexplored areas of armaments innovation nor stocks of conventional (non-nuclear) weapons from mounting unabated. Readers may therefore wish to bear in mind that the theme that seems to emerge from the sixteen articles in this volume is the inexorable movement toward a nuclear devastation despite all the efforts to limit, control or manage the tools of destruction.

None of this is meant to belittle the valiant human attempts, as typified by the SALT II treaty, to call an end to the race for more and more arms. The current annual world expenditure on arms is estimated at more than $400 billion and it is rising. Not surprisingly, it is rising fastest in such regions of instability as the Middle East; less obvious is the fact that it is expected to rise rapidly in the United States as well, whether the Senate ratifies the SALT II agreement or not.

The issues involved in arms control and disarmament are clearly among the most critical facing mankind today. How real is the threat posed by large stocks of conventional and nuclear weapons? Can nuclear weapons be limited? Can their spread among nations be controlled? Is America's security strengthened or weakened by agreements such as SALT? What should American policy be toward arms control and disarmament? These are among the key questions touched on in this volume.

The first section of this compilation provides a general overview of the current arms race, an assessment of the threat posed by nuclear weapons—far and away the most costly and dangerous single element in the global arms race—and an account of the struggle, under way since 1945, to bring them under control. The section includes a description of the international effort in the 1920s and 1930s to limit naval power, and the consequences of that effort.

Part two is given over to articles by writers who favor the SALT II accord, while Part three presents authors who argue the case against the accord. The final section of this compilation looks beyond the debate on SALT II to both the most basic issues of arms control, which remain unresolved, and the prospects for the future.

The compiler wishes to thank the authors and publishers who have courteously granted permission for the reprinting of their materials. He is especially indebted to Denise M. Williams for her able assistance in the preparation of the manuscript.

WILLIAM P. LINEBERRY

September 1979

CONTENTS

I. THE RACE FOR ARMS: WINNERS AND LOSERS

EDITOR'S INTRODUCTION

This may be the only race in which the whole world ends up losing. As the articles in this section make clear, the arms race is a recent contest and has probably collected more players than any other global competition. Its costs stagger the imagination, exceeding the total incomes of more than one hundred of the world's poorest countries. Since all efforts to stuff the nuclear genii back into the bottle have long since been abandoned as hopeless, the goal these days seems to be to limit nuclear weapons development along the lines that would prove least costly to the two key players, the U.S. and the U.S.S.R. In the meantime, however, new players have been joining the nuclear contest, and not even the acknowledged leaders appear to be in any position to win a nuclear showdown.

The first article in this section, an updated report by Kurt Waldheim, Secretary-General of the United Nations, details in vivid terms the extent, costs, and dangers of the worldwide arsenal as it exists today. Is it history, technology, or human frailty that has brought the race to this point? The Secretary-General leaves no doubt in assigning blame. "The primary engine of this worldwide arms race," he observes, "is constituted by the qualitative arms race among the largest military powers. This is due chiefly to the virtual monopoly of these powers in development of advanced military technology, to their overwhelmingly large share of world production and world exports of advanced weaponry and to the global character of their interests, politically and militarily."

9

In the second article, a writer for *Editorial Research Reports* describes the international efforts and incentives to limit nuclear weapons from the end of World War II through SALT I (1972). Another author in the *Nation,* reviewing this same post-war period, concludes that our present "win syndrome" involves what he calls "an impersonal system in which scientists and engineers develop new horror instruments without letup; a host of constituencies, with a material or ideological stake in militarism—to promote those weapons, and a vulgar type of anti-communism to seduce the public into believing it is necessary."

In the last article, reprinted from the *Wall Street Journal,* the author cites an unsuccessful attempt to limit naval arms. He points out that arms limitation treaties can defeat their own purpose by encouraging deception and circumvention. Such treaties "lack the flexibility that enables most international agreements to bend with change and be infused with a new political content."

THE GREAT ARMAMENTS BAZAAR: A GLOBAL PERSPECTIVE[1]

Dynamics of the Arms Race

For a number of years now the world has been diverting annually about $350 billion in today's prices to military purposes. The leading six countries in terms of military expenditure [USA, USSR, China, UK, France, Fed. Rep. of Germany] account for three fourths of this total. Altogether 5 to 6 percent of the world's total output of goods and services are diverted to military ends. In individual countries the percentage diversion is mostly in the 2 to 8 percent bracket, although the extremes range from less than 1 percent to over 30 percent.

[1] From updated report entitled "Economic and Social Consequences of the Arms Race and of Military Expenditures," of the Secretary-General of the United Nations. p 5–22. United Nations Publication, no. E.78.IX.1. 1978.

The arms race is increasingly a worldwide phenomenon, and, although its intensity varies markedly between regions, few countries and no major region has stayed out of it. The competition in armaments between the largest military Powers is by far the most important. It involves the greatest diversion of resources, the greatest inherent dangers and constitutes the principal driving force of the worldwide arms race. This competition is even more intense than is suggested by the immense size and the rapid expansion of their arsenals, because it takes place primarily in a qualitative rather than a quantitative dimension, each new generation of weapons being more complex and more destructive than the systems it replaces. In such areas as the Middle East the competition is both quantitative and qualitative. In some other parts of the world the term "arms race" is less appropriate, but in every major region and in the majority of countries the process of expanding and improving military forces appears to be gathering momentum. This is particularly the case in regions where countries are exposed to political, military, and other kinds of pressures, where the rivalries of other Powers lead to involvement or interference, where territories are under foreign occupation and where countries feel their sovereignty and independence to be directly threatened. This in turn may intensify the wider arms race.

This comprehensive character of the arms race is also reflected in its proliferation into the oceans and into space. In the oceans military rivalry has been increasing in recent years, and space has become of paramount importance for the major Powers for a variety of military purposes such as navigation, surveillance, and target identification.

The primary engine of this worldwide arms race is constituted by the qualitative arms race among the largest military Powers. This is due chiefly to the virtual monopoly of these Powers in development of advanced military technology, to their overwhelmingly large share of world production and world exports of advanced weaponry, and to the global character of their interests, politically and militarily. The six main military spenders not only account for three fourths of world military spending, but for practically all military research and development (R and D) and for practically all exports of weapons and military equipment. All significant developments in armaments originate here and spread from here to the rest of the world, with greater or lesser time lags. For many types of conventional weaponry these time lags seem to have diminished in recent years. Meanwhile, as these weapons are being assimilated in the countries at the periphery of the arms race, new generations are under development at the center to supersede them, preparing the ground for a new round of transfer and emulation. Outside of this small number of producing countries, arms races or competitions are substantially and often wholly dependent on external supplies of arms, technicians, and instructors.

National arms-inventories are not published, and for most types of armaments estimates of world stocks of weapons would be quite uncertain, partly because figures are not known for all countries and partly because different models of the same general type of weapon system, supersonic fighter aircraft, say, cannot be added together to give a world total because performance characteristics and the conditions under which they might be used are too diverse. Nevertheless, some rough indications can be given:

The Nuclear Threat

Current stocks of nuclear weapons are sufficient to destroy the world many times over. These weapons and the missiles, aircraft, and artillery to deliver them are constantly being diversified and their performance characteristics improved. The numbers of nuclear warheads in arsenals is not known, but the number of carriers of different types is known with a fair degree of accuracy. From these numbers it can be inferred that in 1974 so-called "strategic" nuclear forces in the United States and the Soviet Union included 10–11,000 thermonuclear warheads deliverable from missiles or bombers. This number has been rising very fast. Nuclear weapons arsenals are also increasing in other nuclear weapons states. Figures given by SIPRI [Stockholm International Peace Research Institute] indicate that the number of missile-deliverable warheads of the two major nuclear Powers increased from about 3,700 in 1970 to nearly 12,000 in 1976, a rise by more than a factor three. Their combined explosive power is believed to be equivalent to 1.3 million Hiroshima-size bombs. With regard to so-called "tactical" nuclear weapons the situation is more uncertain. Their number is believed to be about four times larger than the number of "strategic" nuclear warheads, but their combined explosive power is but a fraction of the latter. According to one source it is equivalent to about 700 million tons of TNT or to some 50,000 Hiroshima-type bombs.

Even though plausible estimates of numbers of major types of conventional weapons such as aircraft, fighting vessels, and tanks could be constructed for most countries, aggregate figures are not very meaningful for the reasons just given. Only for fighting vessels are figures available which attempt to measure the current value of stocks, taking account of the size, vintage and armament of fighting ships and making allowance for technological improvements. Even these estimates are based on assumptions which are open to challenge, and they can provide no more than a crude indication of trends. They indicate that the total number of fighting ships in the world has changed little over the years, although the value of the world stock (in constant dollars) doubled from 1960 to 1970 and rose by a further 30 percent from 1970 to 1976. This pattern appears to be valid for several other types of armaments as well: world stocks reckoned in numbers have remained fearly constant, but in terms of cost and performance world stocks are increasing very rapidly, and, in the 1970s in particular, current models have been spreading very fast to an increasing number of countries. This is true in particular of modern aircraft. Only 13 developing countries had supersonic aircraft in 1965. A decade later that number had risen to 41. Over the past 30 years a few major arms-producing countries together developed and procured over 70 distinct types of interceptors, fighter and attack aircraft and twice as many variants of these types. To this may be added 30 to 40 types or variants cancelled before they went into production. Even after correcting for inflation, the unit price of fighter aircraft has been doubling every 4 to 5 years, rising from about $0.25 million per aircraft (in 1975 prices) during the Second World War to well over $10 million today, reflecting improvements in performance and armament. All aspects of the cost of most modern weapons systems, development, manufacture, operation, and maintenance have risen very sharply.

. . . The distinguishing characteristic of the present arms race is the continuous qualitative change in the weapons and equipment being produced and deployed. It is primarily this feature that gives the arms race its momentum and it immeasurably complicates efforts to stop or control it.

The past decade has seen a continuous stream of new developments in the sphere of nuclear and conventional means of warfare. Because these technological and qualitative changes have not displayed the spectacular, eye-catching qualities which characterized some earlier developments, such as the advent of the atom bomb or of space technology, there is a danger that it may seem as though military technology was remaining relatively unchanged. Such complacency would be entirely unjustified. Recent developments have profoundly influenced military capabilities, worldwide destructive potentials, and strategic conditions, possibilities and doctrines. In several respects, it will be seen later, these developments greatly reduce the perils of the nuclear arms race. In the key respect of technological development and its implications the arms race is today as intense and danger-ridden as it has ever been.

This cannot be the place for an exhaustive enumeration or a full evaluation of the more recent qualitative phenomena in the armaments field. But a few of the more outstanding developments shall be mentioned to indicate to what extreme degree the arms race is now dominated by rapid technological development. It will be seen in particular that, given the high proportion of military expenditure devoted to R and D, the fact that military expenditures for the world as a whole and for some important countries remained relatively stable in recent years in no way implies a relatively stable military situation.

The most important and spectacular aspect of the arms race in the 1960s was the development and the full-scale deployment of intercontinental ballistic missiles (ICBMs) and of submarine-launched missiles (SLBMs), and the associated deployment of satellite surveillance and communication systems. By the end of that decade there was widespread concern that a new, arms-race spiral may result from the development of anti-ballistic missile systems (ABMs) and from counter-measures in the form of increasing numbers of launchers and, more particularly, of increasing numbers of warheads per launcher to saturate ABM systems. The technical form for the latter development is multiple and independently targetable re-entry vehicles (MIRVs).

The first agreements on the limitation of strategic arms between the United States and the Soviet Union (SALT I), signed in May 1972, set ceilings on the number of ABM sites and ICBM and SLBM launchers, not least to prevent this development. They succeeded in halting the deployment of ABM systems. Since 1972 the number of launchers have been increasing and are approaching the agreed ceilings. In 1976, there were in round figures 2,500 ICBMs and 1,400 SLBMs in these two Powers together.

Continued Buildup

. . . The SALT agreement has had positive effects but it is important not to lose sight of the serious inadequacies in this agreement with regard to the limitation of strategic arms. Thus in recent years the arms race in strategic nuclear weapons has increasingly taken a qualitative direction. Vigorous R and D programs on improved ABM systems have been maintained. The SALT agreement as a whole has had no discernible impact on the extent of MIRV deployment. As a result the number of ICBM and SLBM deliverable nuclear warheads has been rising by about 1,000 every year, even though the number of ICBM and SLBM launchers has remained relatively constant since 1972. (This means that the rate of growth of the number of warheads has declined since 1972.)

Moreover, a major post-MIRV innovation is already at an advanced stage of development. This is a maneuverable re-entry vehicle (MARV) which can change direction in the terminal stages of its trajectory. This could make defense against ballistic missile attack more difficult, but in particular, if combined with developments now taking place in terminal guidance systems, it can provide MARVed missiles with pinpoint accuracies of a few tens of meters instead of current accuracies of somewhat less than one kilometer. With such accuracies, the silos now protecting the land-based ICBMs can be destroyed with near certainty with a single warhead at the first attempt. As a result it becomes possible to consider using "strategic" nuclear weapons in new ways. In addition to being a means of massive reprisals against centers of population and industry to serve as a basic deterrent, it becomes possible to think of using ballistic missiles in "counter-force" roles to gain military advantage at the outset of a war by striking at the weapons and military installations of the opponent, or to use them to conduct supposedly "limited" nuclear war. The adoption of doctrines of this kind could greatly enhance the probability of nuclear war.

No less significant are the implications of the deployment of long-range cruise missiles. These weapons, now under development, are best described as small, highly maneuverable, low-flying pilotless aircraft. They can be equipped with a nuclear as well as a conventional warhead. Current models have ranges of several thousand kilometers and accurate guidance systems, which readjust the trajectory at intervals by comparing terrain features with a map. The accuracy is therefore independent of the range. It will be impossible to determine from its geometry alone whether a cruise missile carries a nuclear or a conventional warhead and, within wide limits, what range it may have. Moreover, it is a small and easily concealed vehicle. Future agreements on strategic weapons may thus become very difficult to negotiate because they would be difficult to verify. The cost of the cruise missile will be at least an order of magnitude less than ICBMs, so that in the years to come it will be well within the financial means of the smaller nuclear powers and of many other countries as well. For some time the exorbitant cost of the latest types of nuclear weapons carriers (ICBMs and SLBMs) has helped maintain the two main military Powers in a class by themselves. In the foreseeable future the importance of this factor may greatly diminish.

Developments in nuclear weapons technology proper are equally ominous, particularly the development of small, low-yield nuclear weapons, of enhanced radiation weapons and of tactical concepts for their use in battle. Delivered with higher accuracy and causing less collateral damage per warhead, their use on the battlefield may seem more acceptable, so that the step from non-nuclear to nuclear war may be more readily taken. Once they are used on the battlefield, escalation towards full-scale nuclear war becomes a dangerous possibility.

The aggregate effect of these developments cannot be understood in terms of the gradual improvements in performance which have been so much a feature of the 1960s that they are hardly news any more. The importance of the changes now underway in the field of nuclear armaments and their carriers is not that their performance in missions traditionally assigned to them is improving year by year, but that essentially new types of missions are becoming possible. New technologies open the way for new doctrines. These in turn give an appearance of rationality to the deployment of weaponry embodying these technologies. At the same time they increase the dangers of war and alter the terms of the disarmament equation, rendering it more complex and more intractable.

Developments in the military use of space have been an essential concomitant, in fact a necessary precondition, for some of these changes. These developments have been overshadowed in the public mind by civilian space exploits. Yet they have been of decisive importance for developments both in nuclear and in so-called "conventional" warfare. In the Indo-China war satellites were used for communication, for weather forecasting prior to bombing raids and for navigation for naval bombardment, but only now are the full potentialities of these means materializing. Satellite technology is having a decisive impact in at least three fields, conferring substantial superiority on the major military Powers:

(a)   Target identification, navigation, and damage assessment in connexion with counterforce strategies in nuclear warfare,

(b)   Surveillance, target identification, and navigation in "conventional" warfare, and

(c)   Worldwide intelligence and surveillance of the military programs of other countries and of wars in which the major Powers are not directly involved.

Potentially, the consequences of this latter capability could be both positive and negative: verification of agreements on arms limitations or disengagement, on the one hand, and area policing and assistance in aggression, on the other. Citing once more an American example because these are the best known, the NAVSTAR program may serve to indicate what is becoming possible in just one field. It is a

24-satellite system which is to provide three-dimensional positioning throughout the world to within about 10 meters. Among its many possible uses is the guidance of both nuclear and non-nuclear forces in so-called "strategic" roles and on the battlefield. It is to be established over the period 1977–1984 at a cost in the $3 billion range. Not only will it allow perfectly accurate guidance of ballistic missiles against fixed targets, an essential component of the counter-force strategy already mentioned, it is also likely to enhance greatly the effectiveness of sea, ground, and air forces in conventional warfare and local wars. Many of these military developments come out of civilian space programs, and in fact the two are not readily separable. In technical terms MIRV was a direct descendant of multiple satellite launching systems, much as maneuvering and docking techniques are at once ancestors and offspring of anti-satellite weapons being developed and tested.

Nuclear Proliferation

The proliferation of nuclear technologies continues at an accelerating pace. France and China, it was mentioned in the 1971 report, acquired a nuclear weapons capability in the 1960s. In 1974, India, which is not a party to the Non-Proliferation Treaty, conducted a nuclear explosion experiment underground. It was officially termed a peaceful nuclear explosion experiment. This explosion demonstrated how readily and cheaply a small nuclear weapons capability could be derived from a major civilian nuclear program. In other cases a nuclear weapons capability could have been acquired without being demonstrated in a nuclear explosion. Civilian nuclear programs, and with them, to a variable degree, the technical expertise and the fissile material required for military programs have spread all over the world during the 1970s. In 1975, 19 countries had nuclear power plants in operation, and another 10 countries will have them by 1980. Experimental reactors are now in operation in well over 50 countries. As far as most industrialized and several developing countries are concerned, there are no longer serious technological or economic barriers against initiating a nuclear weapons program. The only barriers to horizontal proliferation are now political: obligations assumed under the Non-Proliferation Treaty, the good sense of governments and the example to be set in the coming years by the nuclear weapons Powers in agreeing to reduce their own nuclear arsenals. It is, of course, the continuation of the nuclear arms race, not by itself the spread of peaceful uses of nuclear energy, which endangers peace. Stocks of nuclear weapons and the continuation of the nuclear arms race are factors which encourage horizontal nuclear weapons proliferation. The danger of the proliferation of nuclear weapons can be removed by outlawing and halting the production of such weapons and by proceeding to destroy them. The resolutions of the United Nations General Assembly have repeatedly emphasized that the Non-Proliferation Treaty should become universal. It is consequently important to carry out the system of control envisaged in article III of the Non-Proliferation Treaty and that the parties to the Treaty conclude the safeguards agreements with the International Atomic Energy Agency envisaged in article III of the Treaty.

Advances in Conventional Weapons

Also as regards conventional weapons developments have been far-reaching. Throughout the 1960s conventional weapons systems underwent continual and rapid refinement in terms of size, speed, propulsion, fire-power, accuracy, and so forth. Unit costs for major weapons systems typically doubled in real terms during this period. For aircraft it was noted they doubled about twice as fast. Sophisticated weaponry, including supersonic aircraft, became commonplace in the armories of industrialized as well as less developed countries. These developments continued unabated through the period under review. In addition, technological advances in several areas have been combined to produce new types of conventional weapons with potentially far-reaching military and political implications.

New precision guided munitions (PGMs), remotely piloted vehicles (RPVs) and other devices have been developed to carry a conventional warhead to its target with hit probabilities close to 1, or, in the case of RPVs, for reconnaissance and similar missions. This group of weapons is a whole family of devices using the latest developments in such fields as laser technology, microelectronics, electromagnetic sensors in the radar, infrared and optical ranges and wide-band data links for a variety of remote or automatic guidance and/or homing devices. A first generation of PGMs made their appearance in the Indo-China war. In the Middle East in 1973, the enormous potential of such weapons against tanks and aircraft was demonstrated. Both the type of technology involved and their cost make PGMs accessible to many countries, and, indeed, many have them now in their inventories.

Such precision munitions are expected to have battle-field implications no less far-reaching than anything which has happened since the Second World War. The design and mission assignment of the classical weapons carriers, aircraft, ships and tanks, and even the preponderant place they have had hitherto in contemporary armories might be radically changed. The new weapons, together with developments in such areas as night vision devices, battlefield surveillance and communications, are likely to accelerate the pace of modern warfare and to place a still higher premium on standing military forces. Last but not least, with dramatic improvements in accuracy, the yield of the explosive charge becomes a less important parameter in performance. There have been suggestions, for example, that some of the missions now assigned to "tactical" nuclear weapons could be performed by precision-delivered weapons with a conventional warhead. In principle this could mean that military planners would be more willing to dispense with the use of nuclear weapons in a limited conflict, but in practice it could equally well have the effect of blurring the distinction between the use of nuclear and nonnuclear weapons, thus enhancing the risk that an armed conflict develops into nuclear war.

A range of new weapons and munitions based on blast, fragmentation, and incendiary effects has been developed, and was used, notably during the Indo-China war, for saturation bombing over large areas. Such carpet-bombing techniques approach nuclear weapons as regards the blind, indiscriminate destruction they cause, the long-term ecological effects to which they give rise, and the high proportion of wounded and maimed among casualties. Other weapons of massive and indiscriminate destruction have not lagged behind. The effectiveness of incendiary weapons has been considerably increased, and the development of binary nerve gases and their munitions (which are relatively innocuous to handle as the nerve gas is only assembled in flight) could seriously weaken the remaining technical and operational constraints on the deployment of chemical weapons.

Significant developments have also taken place in a number of other fields such as radar technology, anti-submarine warfare techniques, low-altitude interceptor aircraft, laser-guided cannon, and many more.

This rapid technological change originates in a few countries, but it readily spreads to the rest of the world through the transfer of arms, whether in the form of grants or of trade. The rate of innovation and obsolescence in weaponry which is determined by the R and D efforts of the leading countries thus imposes itself on other countries, even though there may be time-lags, depending on the weapons and countries involved. This tendency for the rate of innovation of the leading countries to be transmitted to other countries and regions is already implied by the fact that it is overwhelmingly the technologically leading countries which are the big arms exporters. The six main military spenders, who together account for virtually all military R and D outlays, account for over 90 percent of all military exports and for 95 percent of the exports of major weapons to developing countries. In areas such as the Middle East where the latest developments in conventional weaponry have, particularly in recent years, appeared with little or no time-lag, this process is particularly clear.

The qualitative character of the arms race at its center is thus one of the principal forces behind the accelerating horizontal proliferation of "conventional" weaponry. In addition to the constant pressure on importing countries to modernize their stocks of weapons and equipment, the qualitative character of the arms race gives rise to various pressures in the main producing countries to raise exports, including the need to dispose of obsolete inventories, to achieve large-scale economies, and to lengthen production runs in order to lower unit costs and finance further research and development efforts.

Who Buys Arms?

The total value of transfers of military goods and services cannot be determined with accuracy, although several institutions now publish counts and estimates of arms transfers on a regular basis. The United States Arms Control and Disarmament Agency, which gives the most comprehensive figures, estimates the total value of goods actually delivered in 1975 at $9.7 billion in current prices. This excludes training, services and construction which, if figures for the United States are a valid guide, would add another 30 percent to the total, raising the figure for the value of military goods and services transferred worldwide in 1975 to an estimated $13 billion.

About one third of the total is traded among industrialized countries; another third, approximately, is made up of exports to oil-exporting developing countries, mainly in the Middle East, and the remaining third goes to all other developing countries together. The total value of arms transfers has been growing steadily over the years, increasing by 3 to 4 percent over the past decade if the exceptionally large transfers of 1972 and 1973, mostly related to the wars in Indo-China and the Middle East, are disregarded.

Despite this appearance of continuity, very important changes in the pattern of arms transfers have in fact taken place in this period. First, there has been a rapid rise in the export of major weapons to a number of developing countries and in some cases these are increasingly highly sophisticated weapons. According to SIPRI estimates, exports of major weapons to developing countries rose from $3 billion in 1970 to $6.3 billion in 1975 and $7.3 billion in 1976. Second, there has been a major shift towards transactions on commercial or near-commercial terms. This increasingly commercial character of the market is closely related to a number of other features of the flow of arms in the mid-1970s which contrast markedly with those of arms transfers in the 1960s. While the flow of second-hand and surplus equipment remains important, an increasing part of the arms trade involves the latest models. In some cases export orders have even taken precedence over supplies to the armed forces of the exporting country itself. At the same time, the tendency for each recipient country to have to rely on a single supplier is becoming less pronounced. Prospective buyers are now often the object of active sales efforts by a number of potential suppliers. Again, the commercial character of the market finds expression in the fact that arms transfers are not almost exclusively a function of the pattern of alliances and alignments as they mostly were in the 1960s and earlier. Many countries are now acquiring weapons from other than traditional suppliers and on the basis of what they feel they need for their own purposes. While the supply of arms obviously remains one of the principal means of gaining influence or of keeping out rival political influence, the diplomatic leverage involved in arms transfers is apparently diminishing.

These developments in the direction of greater emphasis on up-to-date equipment, greater military and political autonomy for the recipients vis-à-vis suppliers in a number of cases and more intense competition among the latter could have far-reaching political and military consequences. They have led to growing concern and to efforts to find means of regulating this aspect of the arms race. Particularly in recent years, when some specific deals have attracted such public attention, arms transfers have been a very visible part of the arms race. Nevertheless, it must be borne in mind that arms transfers are only one part of the over-all process of arms acquisition. At about $13 billion annually, arms transfers account for 3 to 4 percent of world military expenditures, or, it may be assumed, for somewhere between 10 and 15 percent of the military equipment produced throughout the world. It follows that rapid expansion in armaments is, with a few notable exceptions, overwhelmingly concentrated in the main arms producing countries, in other words in arms exporting rather than in arms importing countries.

Given that the possession of arms cannot remain the prerogative of a few countries, the realistic alternatives to trade in arms, if the arms race between the main Powers is allowed to go on, are not necessarily preferable to it: arms grants tend to foster relationships of dependence, while domestic arms production is in most cases more costly and could give rise to patterns of dependence between countries and to vested interests within them which are stronger and more lasting than those resulting from arms transfers on commercial terms. Because arms transfers are only a very small part of the total process of arms acquisition, it is not an aspect of the arms race which lends itself to broad and general restraining measures unless such measures are co-ordinated with general progress towards disarmament, involving the arms producing countries as well. Even so, there is urgent need to consider measures aimed at specific regions or weapons systems to avoid encouraging international conflict and to pre-empt costly and pointless local arms races, but without jeopardizing the security of states. There is scope for the exercise of a maximum of self-restraint by countries individually and reciprocally, for collective arrangements on a regional basis or for multilateral negotiations to link regional regulations on types or levels of armaments with measures of disengagement by outside powers, and in some cases for collective action by the international community to deny arms supplies to particular countries.

Qualitative Implications

The strong qualitative momentum of the current arms race has a number of important consequences for the way it develops, the insecurity it generates and in terms of the possibilities for disarmament. In an arms race where the emphasis is on quantity, where technological development is slow and of little consequence, countries may be expected to match their armament efforts to the stocks or the growth rates of the military forces of their opponents. There is room for saturation levels or for mutually agreed ceilings and reductions. Under conditions of rapid military innovation, on the other hand, the decisive factor in the military procurement plans of countries at the forefront of the technological arms race is not so much the actual military strength of their opponents but rather those technological advances which opponents might be able to achieve over the next decade or so (10 years being the typical gestation period for a major technological advance). Inevitably, as the apprehensions of military planners shift from the force levels towards the R and D efforts of their opponents, it is increasingly on the R and D efforts of their own country, which are known, that they will have to base their plans.

In an arms race where the stress is on technological advances the process of weapon and counter-weapon development therefore tends to become in some measure an *intra*-national process, in some cases, only marginally related to the stages actually reached by other countries. Each country is actively seeking means of defeating its own most advanced weapons and of neutralizing its own most recent defenses, thus conferring on the development of military technology a momentum and a rate of obsolescence much greater than in comparable civilian applications. A qualitative arms race with its long lead time and its emphasis on future possibilities rather than current realities tends to move in one direction only: one country's advances in weaponry will be emulated by others, but its self-restraint need not be. Similarly an increase in international tension may accelerate the arms race, but an improvement of the international climate will not necessarily suffice to slow it down.

In advanced military technology, the achievement of exacting technical specifications and early delivery schedules tend to take precedence over cost considerations when new weapons are being designed. The large cost-overruns which have become an almost normal feature of advanced military projects illustrate this fact. The result is an increasing volume of research and development with each new generation of weapons. For example it is estimated that the number of draftsmen required for the design of a military aircraft today is typically of the order of 4,000 man-years, spread over a 7- to 10-year period. This may be compared with about 170 man-years, spread over 2 to 3 years, required for the design of the Halifax bomber on the eve of the Second World War. For many years now rising R and D requirements have had to be met by expanding the staff rather than lengthening the design cycle, if weapons were not to be already obsolete when they entered into service. This trend towards rapid development and design by means of ever larger teams of engineers, scientists, and technicians which is inherent in a qualitative arms race cannot fail to create problems of surplus capacity both in design and in production unless military procurement expands for every new generation of weapons. Continuous employment is only compatible with rapid development and design if production cycles are short and military stocks are replaced at a rapid rate. The abandonment of many advanced weapons programs before production started but after hundreds of millions of dollars had been spent on development, again a recurrent feature of the past decades, has of course helped to alleviate somewhat this problem of surplus capacity. Even disregarding the inherently wasteful character of weapons themselves, arms production under the conditions of a qualitative arms race appears as an exceptionally wasteful process, whatever the form in which the waste appears: as project cancellations half-way through, as intermittent underemployment or as military arsenals which are allowed to expand for industrial rather than military reasons.

Causes of the Arms Race

The forces behind an ever-expanding arms race and the intense development and exploitation of technology for military purposes cannot be accounted for simply in terms of action-reaction processes, of the apprehension raised in each country by the military programs of others. As the arms race expands in the direction of ever-greater reliance on advanced technology and draws into its orbit ever new sectors of society, a number of new mechanisms set in which tend to perpetuate the race if not to accelerate it. The sheer logic of technological innovation, the fact that one cannot apparently afford to leave any avenue unexplored, the industrial imperative and other implications of long lead times have already been mentioned. A number of other factors have been proposed to explain the blind momentum and the vast scale which characterize the present arms race. In addition to a variety of more or less explicit political and military motivations applicable to individual cases, a number of domestic factors may be involved. Their importance obviously depends on the precise circumstances. In some instances, the armed forces have been expanding mainly in response to internal strains and have served to uphold the social order in the face of mounting opposition or of profound divisions in society. Another factor is the inertia inherent in institutions once established and consolidated and in the coalitions of interest which may develop between the armed forces, industry, sectors of the scientific and technological professions and political and administrative apparatuses. Some studies of specific decisions on military procurement have emphasized the important roles played by compromise arrangements between different institutional and bureaucratic pressures, on the one hand, and by inter-service rivalries, on the other.

A thorough understanding of these several processes which sustain the arms race and determine its orientation is, of course, an essential prerequisite if political action is to turn the tide. Each of them directly points to forces that may impede progress towards disarmament. So far these different processes are, however, on the whole poorly understood. One important reason is that the same factors and combinations of factors are not at work everywhere. There are evidently great differences between the countries at the technological forefront of the arms race and the countries which are gradually being drawn along, between countries with different socio-economic systems, and so forth. Despite this, studies have had to be confined almost entirely to those countries, the United States and some European countries in particular, for which sufficient information has been available. But if effective progress towards disarmament is to be achieved it will clearly be insufficient to regard the arms race merely as an action-reaction phenomenon, and disarmament as simply a question of political will at the highest decision-making levels. The arms race is not only becoming more dangerous; it is also becoming more complex and more firmly entrenched. It is sustained by a variety of forces acting together, and it must be expected that to remove one of them is not sufficient to reverse its course. In fact, it may be assumed that it is not one or a few single factors but precisely their multiplicity which confers upon the arms race its great inertia and which has rendered it so intractable from the point of view of disarmament, any limited successes in one field tending to be offset very quickly by developments in other sectors of the arms race.

A point to be specially stressed is that in an arms race so consistently bent on qualitative improvements and the quest for achieving or pre-empting technological breakthroughs, a mere inspection of trends in military expenditure gives a wrong impression of the true rise in destructive potential. In civilian production it is a well-known proposition that under conditions of continuous technical progress even a policy of zero net-investment will lead to a constantly increasing output. Worn-out machines are replaced by machines incorporating a more advanced technology and this results in higher productivity. The same applies to military expenditure. Even if it does not rise in real terms, the devotion of a large proportion to R and D and to qualitative improvement means that the destructiveness and the potential danger of the military apparatus continues to grow.

A corollary springing from the observations in the foregoing paragraph is that it is necessary to distinguish between the economic and the military consequences of armaments expenditure. They bear no necessary relationship to one another: a rise in the (real) volume of military expenditure will almost always imply an increase in lethality and destructive power. But when such expenditure is reduced there may well be a divergent movement: a certain relaxation of the over-all economic burden can be accompanied by a further extension of destructive power, as indeed we are witnessing today in some countries. Since, however, the concentration on the qualitative (i.e. technological) arms race requires a high input of specially scarce qualified manpower (scientists, technicians, management, highly-skilled workers), shifts towards greater emphasis on rapid qualitative change can be economically harmful, even when they are accompanied by a reduction in total (real) military expenditure.

The facts about the qualitative character of the arms race—alarming and growing in importance—have to be kept in mind when measures against a continuation of the arms race are discussed. It will not suffice to take cuts in total miltary expenditure as the sole criterion of progress unless they are very substantial indeed. Supporting measures to contain the qualitative arms race are imperative.

The Dimensions of Arms Control

One form of progress consists in setting limits on special weapons and weapon systems. The ABM Agreement between the United States and the USSR or the Biological Disarmament Convention are cases in point. Similar steps over wider ranges of weapons and modes of warfare, nuclear and chemical means of warfare in particular, would help to erect important boundaries for the arms race. To be most effective these measures should be directed at new developments, that is before any significant R and D work has been done and before the projects acquire a political, institutional, and industrial momentum. Provided this does not detract from the primary task of constraining and reversing the nuclear arms race and of abolishing existing weapons, there is also a case for seeking prohibitions of the development and manufacture of new types and systems of weapons of mass destruction, as called for in several resolutions of the General Assembly. The banning of new weapons and systems of mass destruction must be closely linked to firm measures for the cessation of nuclear weapons production, the liquidation of the existing stockpiles and the complete and definitive prohibition of nuclear weapons. A decisive attack on the qualitative arms race would also be achieved if an agreement could be reached among the leading military powers to cut down expenditure on military R and D. Such a measure could also—after redirecting the released resources—lead to important economic and social benefits to both the developed and developing nations.

The commitment to incessant qualitative change is

deeply embedded in the inner logic of the arms race. Agreements on qualitative and technological restrictions are not easily reached, not least because of difficult verification problems. But if the difficulties of securing some measure of control over this dimension of the arms race are particularly great, so too is the urgency of the need to take determined steps in this direction. Each passing year sees the initiation of a spate of new weapons, and existing programs become more deeply entrenched in the military and political systems of countries and thus more difficult to stop.

In the light of the developments described above, it is necessary to expound openly the dangers of the continuation of the arms race, and to dispel illusions that lasting peace and security can coexist with huge accumulations of means of destruction. The adoption and implementation of resolute measures in the field of disarmament and particularly nuclear disarmament, ultimately leading to general and complete disarmament, has become imperative. At the same time it is necessary to intensify efforts for the adoption of partial measures of military disengagement and disarmament that can contribute to the achievement of that goal.

REIGNING IN THE RACE: CONTROLLING NUCLEAR WEAPONS[2]

The attitudes of the United States and the Soviet Union toward nuclear weapons and strategic arms limitation have not changed significantly since the first control proposals were offered more than 30 years ago. Despite changes in the strategic balance and the ensuing American shift from a policy of massive retaliation to one of deterrence during that period, the United States has attempted to ensure its

[2] From pamphlet entitled "Politics of Strategic Arms Negotiations," by Mary Costello, a staff writer. *Editorial Research Reports.* 1:361-7. My. 13, '77. Reprinted by permission.

nuclear superiority as the most effective way of containing the Soviet Union. The Russians, on the other hand, aimed at parity because Soviet leaders felt that without rough equivalence the Soviet Union would be "subject to coercion based on American strategic nuclear superiority."

Mutual fear and distrust led to massive nuclear weapons buildups and discouraged any substantive effort to limit strategic arms until at least the early 1970s. In a 1961 study for the Brookings Institution, Bernard G. Bechhoefer described the numerous proposals and counterproposals between 1946 and 1960 for eliminating or limiting nuclear weapons. On the surface, he wrote, "the 15 years of negotiations have resulted in a total impasse with no formal agreements of any nature. Except in the field of nuclear test cessation, the great powers cannot even decide on procedures for resuming negotiations."

The Baruch Plan

The first American proposal for controlling nuclear weapons was presented to the United Nations Atomic Energy Commission by Bernard M. Baruch, chairman of the U.S. delegation to the commission, on June 14, 1946. The Baruch plan called upon the United States and other nations to transfer to an international authority ownership and control of all atomic materials and activities. The proposal also stipulated that all countries refrain from manufacturing atomic weapons and that those already possessing them destroy them once the international authority had been established. That agency was to have an unrestricted right to conduct inspections.

The Soviet Union rejected the Baruch proposal for two main reasons. First, it required the Russians to trust the United States with sole possession of nuclear weapons until international control was set up at some unspecified time in the future. In 1946 the Soviet Union was still in the early stages of developing its own atomic weapons. The second reason was that the plan required each country to allow inspections in its territory, something the Russians have never permitted.

Soviet Proposals on Arms Control

The Russians challenged the Baruch proposal with a host of objections and a few plans of their own. One of the first Soviet plans, presented by Gromyko five days after the Baruch plan was announced, called for the destruction of all nuclear weapons before the international agency was set up and a total prohibition on the use of atomic weapons. The numerical superiority of Soviet conventional forces made this proposal unacceptable to American and European leaders. Talks on arms control continued, but it was not until after Stalin's death in 1953 and Nikita Khrushchev's stress on peaceful coexistence that talks seemed to be getting anywhere.

On May 10, 1955, the Russians put forth a proposal to the UN Disarmament Commission in New York that appeared consistent with a 1954 Western plan. They called for a reduction in armed forces and military expenditures; after 75 percent of the scheduled reductions had been carried out, there would be a complete ban on production, possession, and use of atomic weapons. At the Geneva summit conference two months later, President Eisenhower advanced an "open skies" proposal requiring both countries to make facilities available to each other for aerial reconnaissance and to exchange blueprints for each other's military installations.

The Russians branded the open skies plan "nothing but a bald espionage plot." But until September 6 of that year there was some hope that a major disarmament agreement could be reached. On that date, Harold E. Stassen, Eisenhower's Special Assistant on Disarmament, announced that since there was no reliable inspection system, the United States was withdrawing all its previous proposals. There has been considerable speculation about why Stassen negated all past U.S. disarmament plans; one observer noted: "Some critics believe that Washington pulled back because agreement suddenly seemed within reach."

There is a question as to whether the United States was sincerely interested in disarmament during a period when it enjoyed vast nuclear superiority. Until 1960, when Eisenhower created a special Disarmament Agency within the Department of State, this country had not set up a permanent staff to study arms control problems and formulate policy. To overcome the criticism that the National Planning Association leveled at U.S. disarmament efforts in a 1960 report, Congress made the Disarmament Agency independent of the State Department and changed its name to the Arms Control and Disarmament Agency in 1961. The new agency was charged with responsibility for conducting research, preparing policy recommendations, and participating in disarmament negotiations.

Long Negotiations Over Limits on Testing

The difficulties in reaching a strategic arms agreement were evident in the long and arduous negotiations to limit nuclear-weapons testing. As early as 1954, Indian Prime Minister Jawaharlal Nehru had urged a suspension of tests. The Russians called for a halt in their disarmament proposal of May 10, 1955. In the years that followed, each superpower temporarily suspended its own testing but there was no international agreement. Public concern about the health hazards of radioactive fallout from the tests increased.

There were several reasons why neither the United States nor the Soviet Union was willing to agree to a test-ban treaty until 1963, and then only to a partial suspension of testing. One was Russian opposition to on-site inspection. Another was that a ban on testing could be viewed as a back-door approach to total nuclear disarmament. Henry A. Kissinger, then a professor at the Harvard Center for International Affairs, took note of this connection in an article in the October 1958 issue of *Foreign Affairs:* "If a cessation of nuclear testing is a 'first step' to anything, it is to an increased campaign to outlaw nuclear weapons altogether."

"Unilateral initiatives designed to promote progress in arms control are sometimes difficult to distinguish from efforts to gain propaganda advantages," the Arms Control and Disarmament Agency has observed. "There had been unilateral offers, first by the Soviet Union and later by the United States and the United Kingdom, to suspend nuclear testing, but these offers came after the parties had just completed extensive nuclear tests. Not too surprisingly, the self-serving offers were not reciprocated. Then, on November 7, 1958, President Eisenhower announced that the United States would continue its suspension of testing despite the most recent Soviet tests, and a self-imposed moratorium began." The moratorium was broken when the Russians resumed testing in August 1961; the United States began testing again the next spring.

Despite overtures from Khrushchev, President Kennedy ordered a buildup of ICBMs soon after taking office. This was partly to counter what he perceived as a "missile gap," a phrase he introduced in his presidential election campaign. It was not until after the Cuban missile crisis of October 1962 that the two sides were able to resume serious negotiations on testing. A limited test-ban treaty ending experimental nuclear weapons tests in the atmosphere, outer space, and under water was signed by the United States, Russia and Britain in August 1963. Over 110 other countries now are signers of the treaty.

Regardless of its benefits, the test-ban treaty was hardly a breakthrough in arms control or reduction. Both sides proceeded to conduct their testing underground; the United States carried out more nuclear tests (469) in the 10 years after the test ban than it had in the previous 18 years (424 tests). To win approval of the treaty in the Senate, where the Joint Chiefs of Staff had enlisted several powerful opponents, Kennedy was forced to offer some safeguards.

Strategic Buildups and Concern in 1960s

The American strategic buildup that began two years before the treaty was signed continued for the rest of the decade. The number of ICBMs was substantially increased, submarine-launched Polaris missiles were developed, supersonic fighter-bombers were ordered and, by 1965, contracts had been given to Boeing for work on MIRV. The Soviet reaction to the American buildup was, predictably, an escalation of their own strategic weapons programs.

The Russian buildup focused on ICBMs and anti-ballistic missile (ABM) defense systems. In 1966, for example, the Soviet Union had only about one-third as many ICBMs (250) as the United States. Two years later, according to U.S. estimates, the Russains had 900. Despite the outcry in this country over the Soviet buildup, the following comparison of strategic arsenals released by Secretary of Defense Clark M. Clifford on October 25, 1968, indicated the United States still enjoyed a sizable overall lead:

Weapons	United States	Soviet Union
Deliverable warheads	4,206	1,200
Launchers:		
Land-based ICBMs	1,054	900
Intercontinental bombers	646	150-155
Sea-launched missiles	656	75-80

A number of factors prevented serious consideration of strategic weapons reduction: the growing American involvement in Vietnam; the Soviet invasion of Czechoslovakia in August 1968; and a large strategic buildup then under way in Russia. Nevertheless, two multilateral agreements on nuclear weapons were signed in the late 1960s: a 1967 treaty banning the orbiting of devices equipped with nuclear weapons and a 1968 treaty on the non-proliferation of atomic weapons.

During his years in office, President Johnson suggested several plans for nuclear arms limitation. Behind many of these proposals was growing American concern about the Russian ABM program. A Soviet breakthrough in missile defense technology would, if not matched by the West, overcome this country's advantage in offensive weaponry. By making its territory immune to American missiles, the Soviet Union could attack the United States without fear of retaliation. The choice facing Johnson and later President Nixon was either to begin building a multibillion-dollar ABM system or to persuade the Russians to discard their ABM defenses.

At a "summit meeting" between Johnson and Premier Aleksei N. Kosygin in 1967 at Glassboro, N.J., Secretary of Defense Robert S. McNamara unsuccessfully urged the Soviet leader to abandon the ABM in order to hold back an arms race. McNamara opposed the development of American anti-ballistic missiles as too costly, possibly ineffective and certain to provoke escalation of the arms race. But faced with Russia's refusal to limit its system, the Pentagon announced late in 1967 that the United States would deploy a limited ABM system called Sentinel. Soon after taking office in 1969, Nixon asked Congress for a "thin" system called Safeguard. Congress, by the narrowest of margins, acceded to Nixon's request that August.

Proponents of the use of "bargaining chips" often cite the U.S. decision to proceed with ABM development as the key element in Soviet acceptance of limits on the system in the 1972 SALT I treaty. Others argue that the ABM buildup was unnecessary. By 1972, they contend, both sides had come to the conclusion that their costly systems were ineffective. The American system was directed primarily against an improbable attack from the Chinese and, according to Edgar M. Bottome [author, *Balance of Terror*], the Soviet system was virtually "worthless" against a U.S. nuclear attack.

A combination of events and new thinking led to the opening of strategic arms limitation talks in 1969—fear that the strategic arms race was growing out of control, Soviet economic problems, U.S. concessions on international inspection, and American acknowledgement that a situation of rough nuclear parity existed between the two superpowers. The notion of superpower parity was particularly important, Professor James E. Dougherty [teacher, international relations] wrote, because this was the first time in the nuclear era "that such a condition has been thought to exist."

Nixon and Kissinger Approach to SALT I

In addition to acknowledging superpower parity, the Nixon-Kissinger policy on SALT was characterized by the overriding importance given to broadly political—as opposed to technical—aspects of strategic arms negotiations. An agreement on nuclear weapons was perceived as one link in overall U.S.-Soviet relations that would, in Kissinger's words, add to the "momentum of détente" and facilitate the achievement of global "stability."

In his first press conference as President, on January 27, 1969, Nixon indicated the "linkage" between SALT and other aspects of U.S.-Soviet relations. "What I want to do is to see to it that we have strategic talks in a way and at a time that will promote, if possible, progress on outstanding political problems . . . in which the United States and the Soviet Union, acting together, can serve the cause of peace." Kissinger, apparently upset that Nixon publicly linked progress on SALT to Russian action elsewhere, issued "clarifications" that one was not necessarily dependent on the other. Nevertheless, for the next eight years, détente was premised on such "linkages."

The SALT I agreement in May 1972 came under increasing criticism from both hawks and doves. Hawks complained that the United States made unnecessary concessions merely to foster an illusion of détente; doves chided the administration for failing to reach an agreement that reduced the number of strategic weapons. Both were unhappy about the secrecy and, some said, deception that had characterized American diplomacy. To reduce opposition in the Senate to the SALT treaty, the administration accepted an amendment sponsored by Sen. Henry M. Jackson that in future arms agreements the United States accept nothing less than equality in intercontinental weapons systems.

The Vladivostok guidelines embodied this equality feature but failed to satisfy critics. Both liberals and conservatives complained that the ceilings were unnecessarily high and that Vladivostok, like SALT I, failed to meet even the minimal arms-control objectives: reducing the danger of war and the burden of defense expenditures. While supporters of the agreements might well argue that both decreased the likelihood of war, it is undeniable that neither SALT I nor Vladivostok curtailed strategic weapons spending.

THIRTY YEARS OF ESCALATION[3]

Since 1945, American, Soviet, and other diplomats have met at least 6,000 times to discuss "disarmament" and its illegitimate offspring, "arms control," but in thirty-two years not a single weapon has been eliminated by mutual agreement. On the contrary, the arms race—conventional and nuclear, but especially nuclear—has escalated relentlessly, with the two superpowers now in possession of firepower two million times greater than all the bombs, grenades, and bullets used in World War II. And by now we have entered what is called the "second nuclear age"—the age of plutonium and proliferation—in which forty nations will have the capability of producing nuclear bombs by 1985 and 100 by the year 2000. In light of these developments many experts predict that nuclear war is both imminent and inevitable.

[3] Article by Sidney Lens, contributing editor of *The Progressive* and author of *The Day Before Doomsday*. Nation. 226:622-6. My. 27, '78. Reprinted by permission.

So, why doesn't somebody stop the arms race?

Beginning with Harry Truman, every President has spoken of the ultimate need to achieve, in Carter's words, "zero nuclear weapons." Yet every President has added to the stockpile, both quantitatively and qualitatively. Truman proposed the Baruch plan for world disarmament, but continued to produce atom bombs and in 1949 ordered development of the hydrogen (fusion) bomb, whose explosive force is in the range of millions of tons of TNT equivalent, rather than thousands of tons, as in the fission bomb —or ten tons, as in the World War II "blockbuster." Eisenhower spoke of "atoms for peace" at the much-heralded December 1953 UN meeting, but put the H-bomb into production and pioneered two major escalations in the arms race, the missile and the nuclear submarine.

Proposing a "program for general and complete disarmament" in the fall of 1961, Kennedy asserted that "mankind must put an end to war—or war will put an end to mankind. . . . The risks inherent in disarmament pale in comparison to the risks inherent in an unlimited arms race." But soon thereafter he asked Congress to add $6 billion to the military budget. And so it goes. The cost of "defense" has skyrocketed from $12 billion in 1948, to $80 billion in 1973, to $128 billion [in 1979]; it is projected at $173 billion by the end of Carter's first term.

Conventional wisdom has it that we must spend such sums (nearly $2 trillion since World War II) to prevent the Russians from "taking us over." This argument has more flaws than a con man's sales pitch. To begin with, the United States initiated the major advances in the nuclear race: the atom bomb (four years before the Russians), the hydrogen bomb (nine months lead), the missile (despite Sputnik), the nuclear sub, the MIRV (Multiple Individually Targeted Re-Entry Vehicle), the MARV (Maneuvering Re-Entry Vehicle), the cruise, the accuracy systems. The United States has always been ahead, and remains far ahead even today when hawks like Paul Nitze are shouting themselves hoarse that "the Russians are out-spending us."

Kill Power

To put the Pentagon's kill power in perspective: the bomb that fell on Hiroshima, August 6, 1945, was a 13-kiloton bomb (equal to 13,000 tons of TNT). [A 1977] study . . . made by an international group of scientists and based on recently declassified material put the deaths from that one bomb at 140,000. The U.S. arsenal of 9,000 strategic and 22,000 tactical warheads is now equal to 620,000 Hiroshima-type bombs. Or, put another way, it is enough to kill every Russian (if instantly reincarnated) thirty-six times, and every person on earth twelve times. And we continue to produce three warheads a day. The Soviets have heavier weapons (in part because some are still liquid-fueled) but they are about half as accurate (a decisive weakness when it comes to what is called "lethality"), and about one-third as numerous—4,500 strategic and 7,000 tactical, a total of 11,500, as against our 31,000.

And even if the Soviets were as strong as our hawks assert, the argument for more weapons would be a hoax. The government claims to pursue a strategy of "deterrence," of stalemate, or "balance of terror"—what Secretary Robert McNamara called "Mutual Assured Destruction" (MAD). The theory is that, since each side has enough deliverable warheads to assure the destruction of the other as a viable society, no matter who strikes first, both are safe. Neither will dare (unless its leaders go berserk or there is an accident) to initiate a nuclear war.

But while MAD is the *stated* policy of the government, it is not the actual policy. Consider: there are in the USSR 218 cities with a population of 100,000 or more, and 218 medium-sized warheads can destroy those cities as functioning entities, especially if launched from nuclear submarines, which cannot be tracked down or destroyed under present anti-submarine technologies available to the Russians.

Hence, a single Poseidon submarine, carrying sixteen missiles, each with ten to fourteen warheads (a total of 160 to 224), can make a shambles of the Soviet Union's urban centers. Allowing for misfires, certainly two Poseidons are more than enough to guarantee McNamara's formula for "assured destruction," defined by him as "one-fifth to one-fourth of the Soviet population and one-half of her industrial capacity." The United States has thirty-one Poseidons, plus ten older Polaris submarines, and is now building the modern Trident, with double the capacity of the Poseidons. If "deterrence" or MAD is our goal, why this immense firepower, why this excess kill capability?

We obviously achieved a stage of "assured destruction" at least a decade ago. McNamara himself made that point in a September 1967 speech, asserting that both superpowers now possessed "strategic nuclear arsenals greatly in excess of credible assured destruction capability." The estimates used by McNamara and the Pentagon since the late 1960s are 95 million to 120 million dead on each side in a nuclear confrontation, plus three-quarters of the industry destroyed. Even earlier, after the October 1962 Cuban missile crisis, Kennedy put the matter more graphically: if the war between the two superpowers had broken out then, he said, everything that the United States had worked so hard to build in 300 years would have been destroyed in eighteen hours. "Even the fruits of victory" would have been "ashes in our mouths."

Moreover, the *type* of weapons the United States is now developing hints at something other than simple "deterrence." The cruise missile, when deployed, will hit within 15 to 30 yards of a target 2,000 miles away. The MARV, the Mark 12-A warhead and other wonder weapons are also incredibly accurate at long distances. The point is that weapons that are accurate are not necessary for a "second strike" retaliatory attack on cities and populations. A bomb that can come within a half mile or so of its target is more than adequate for simple "deterrence." Accuracy becomes important, however, when a nation plans a surprise *first* strike that will deprive the adversary of his response. The greater the accuracy the fewer bombs needed to demolish enemy missile silos *hardened* by thousands of tons of steel and concrete. It is not only the size of the U.S. arsenal, therefore, which indicates that the policy makers have a more ominous purpose than simple "deterrence" but the character of the weapons they are developing.

Beyond Deterrence

The American people are told that their government wants no more than a nuclear stalemate, the capacity to "deter" the Soviet Union. But current plans go far beyond "deterrence," as Secretary of Defense Harold Brown concedes in his latest annual report. "We have to plan our strategic forces," he writes, "on the basis that *deterrence might fail*." (Emphasis added.) In that case, he says, we need "what are so awkwardly called war-fighting forces," forces that can actually win nuclear wars.

That exposes the nub of the problem—what may be called the "win syndrome." Military establishments always plan for victory, but the present "win syndrome" is unique in at least four respects: first, it has coalesced with a technology that makes possible the extinction of all human life; second, it has created a pro-militarist constituency immeasurably more powerful than the old "merchants of death"; third, it must—and does—undermine internal democracy and countervailing power; fourth, and most ominous of all, it gives the arms race a *self-propelling* character—so self-propelling in fact, that no single human being, not even the President, has the power to stop it unless there is a far-reaching public outcry to end the race.

The win syndrome, to put it simply, leads to Armageddon!

Back in 1945–46 many people associated with the government had grave reservations about The Bomb. Hundreds of scientists who had worked on it pleaded that it not be used. Generals Eisenhower, Arnold, and LeMay and Admiral Leahy thought it was a mistake to use it in August 1945. Secretary of War Stimson, who ordered The Bomb dropped in August, had a change of heart in September and urged Truman to form an "atomic partnership" with the Soviets, to forestall an arms race. Bernard Brodie and a group of theorists at Yale wrote that "thus far the chief purpose of our military establishment has been to win wars. From now on, its chief purpose must be to avert them."

But the official Truman family was convinced that mere existence of The Bomb would cause the Soviet Union—the only serious potential adversary—to become pliant. (In the words of British Nobel Laureate, Sir Solly Zuckerman, this is the best type of victory, where "the adversary surrenders without a shot being fired.") Stimson wrote in his diary that the Soviets "can't get along without our help and industries and we have coming into action a weapon which will be unique." Truman himself told a visitor, according to historian William Appleman Williams, "that the Russians would soon be put in their place; and that the United States would then take the lead in running the world in a way that the world ought to be run." Russia was so devastated—20 million dead, more than 70,000 cities and villages destroyed—American leaders believed, according to former State Department official Richard Barnet, that "the Soviet Union was not much of a rival." By applying the right pressures it could be forced to accept the American design for a new world order.

The new world order was a vital factor in relations with the Soviet Union and in the arms race that ensued from those strained relations. It requires some explanation.

U.S. national income had doubled during World War II and its capital equipment industry had grown, according to the National Planning Association, to "nearly twice the size which would be needed domestically." Unless the United States could find foreign markets to absorb the goods this excess capacity produced, it would face a depression on the 1929 scale. It also needed foreign markets for its excess capital, since it was selling about $10 billion of commodities overseas annually and buying only $3.5 billion. The balance of payments was so favorable by the end of the war that the United States had accumulated a stockpile of $29 billion in gold (then worth $35 an ounce) —or 77 percent of the "free world's" total reserves.

Everyone of course wanted American goods, but no one had the money to pay for them; friend and foe alike lay prostrate. Washington's Pax Americana was an economic and military program aimed at solving this dilemma. It was two-pronged:

(1) A system of grants and loans—$170 billion from 1945 to 1975—to stabilize the economies of America's allies and clients. In return, recipients would agree to two major conditions: first, that the American dollar would be the international medium of exchange; second, that they would open their doors to freer trade and equal investment opportunities—to the immense advantage of the United States, which at that time could undersell and outinvest any rival. Britain, for instance, was required to give up its empire preference system and allow U.S. goods and capital to flow into Commonwealth nations on equal terms with its own members. As John F. Kennedy would note, "foreign aid is a method by which the United States maintains a position of influence and control around the world. . . ."

(2) To back up the economic plan, a military program was devised to assure that nations willing to live under Pax Americana would be protected not only from outsiders but most of all from their own people. It made little sense to give aid to a nation that was about to have a revolution and run off into the Communist or neutralist camp. Hence, retaining "friendly" regimes in power was a *sine qua non* of Pax Americana, requiring a Central Intelligence Agency and military machine unparalleled in the history of armaments.

The United States built the biggest navy the world had ever known. It acquired 429 major bases and 2,972 minor ones (before the war it had only a few fueling stations outside its borders) from which it could come rapidly to the aid of harassed allies—either by a "show of force" such as sending ships and/or troops to their ports (something the United States has done on more than 215 occasions since World War II) ; by giving secret military aid; or in extreme instances, by intervening directly, as in Korea, Lebanon, the Dominican Republic and Vietnam.

"There Is No Defense . . ."

Since Truman rejected coexistence with Moscow, the success of Pax Americana depended most of all on a military counterweight to keep the Soviets "in their place." That was required for two reasons, first because it was inevitable that Moscow would support national revolutions in order to reduce the Western sphere of influence; and second, because there was always the possibility that, while the United States was militarily occupied in one place, the Soviets might become adventurous elsewhere. At the outset of the Korean War, for instance, there was considerable anxiety at the Truman White House that the Asian upheaval was a Soviet diversion for an impending attack in Europe. In fact Eisenhower was sent to beef up NATO forces on the Continent for just such a possibility.

There was a major weakness in the preparedness program—defense, *physical* defense—but far from slowing the Pentagon juggernaut, that vulnerability gave it additional momentum. Offensive nuclear weapons can annihilate an adversary many times over, but there is no effective way to defend the United States itself from intolerable "damage," though the military has tried valiantly to find one. In the days of the bomber, before the missile, military officials elaborated a plan for evacuating the big cities—New York, for instance, in fifty hours. This was folly at best—as anyone can attest who has lived through a New York snowstorm—

but it became utter nonsense when the missile made its appearance: missile flight time from Moscow to Washington is thirty minutes. The next theory of defense, advocated by Nelson Rockefeller but implemented by Kennedy, was the fallout-shelter program. According to *Life*, in one of the most fraudulent articles ever written, it would save 97 percent of us. Herman Kahn in the meantime introduced a plan to put the urban population in underground cities—complete with schools, factories, etc.—and then issue an ultimatum to the Russians to surrender (since they could kill only a "few" of us and we could kill most of them). Then there was the campaign during the Johnson and Nixon administrations for an anti-ballistic missile (ABM), which would intercept and destroy an incoming Soviet projectile. All such schemes have proven vain—and expensive. There is no defense, though the researchers are still working on it.

In the absence of defense, or what the Pentagon in its exquisite prose calls "damage-limitation," there was no way to win a *total* nuclear war. The Pentagon persists in its search for the one great wonder weapon that will assure total victory but, meanwhile, the emphasis is on wars of lesser, limited nature—at the level of the CIA, which overthrows and undermines unfriendly governments; at the level of wars by proxy (as in the Middle East), and "small" wars of intervention with conventional weapons (as in Indochina and Korea).

In 1974 Secretary James Schlesinger added a new focus to the "win syndrome"—limited *nuclear* wars. Nuclear war should be made "thinkable" by making it *smaller*, by fighting on a limited scale, so that the adversary is "wounded" instead of "killed." Presumably, after being wounded a sufficient number of times he would give up. The National Security Council has seriously discussed nuclear confrontations on at least eight occasions that we know of, but the Schlesinger doctrine of 1974 was the first time limited nuclear war was *officially* approved. Henceforth the United

States will not shy from using nuclear weapons on a limited front, say in a war with North Korea, or a war in Europe. For this purpose it already has a plethora of tactical weapons, including "mini-nukes" that can be carried in a knapsack; the neutron bomb; nuclear artillery shells and mines, and pilotless drones which seek out the enemy and attack him from far behind the lines.

Meanwhile the hawks in and around the Pentagon continue to promote arms escalation in the hope that sooner or later they will find either a defensive weapon that "limits damage" to tolerable levels, or an offensive weapon that will make possible a *"disarming* first strike."

Originally it was felt that the atom bomb by itself would stay the hand of the Soviet Union and its allies. By 1948–49, however, it was evident that The Bomb lacked the political clout that Washington assigned to it. The United States suffered three stunning setbacks: Benes and Masaryk were overthrown by the Communists in Czechoslovakia, Mao seized power in China, and the Soviets tested their first bomb at least a decade ahead of our schedule for them. The American response was not to re-evaluate the utility of the atom bomb but to order production of the hydrogen bomb. Like compulsive gamblers, ever since then, the response of U.S. leaders to every major crisis or feeling of anxiety has been to put another military chip in the pot. And as the emphasis on militarism grew, the arms race developed what McNamara was to call "a kind of mad momentum intrinsic to the development of all new nuclear weaponry." It became institutionalized, rigid, self-propelling.

Being "Prepared"

Three factors contributed to automatic escalation. First, a rampant technology was developing new weapons—and selling them—with no thought to geopolitical or human consequences. Ralph Lapp, one of the early atomic scientists, noted that the imperative of technology was that "if a weapons system could be made, then it would be made."

The scale of this "mad momentum" can be gauged by the fact that as of 1973 the federal budget was sponsoring 19,000 separate research, development, test and evaluations projects. Members of the scientific community fought like tigers for a piece of Pentagon research and development (R&D) funds, first a few hundred million, then a few billion, now $12 billion or more a year. Scientists, engineers, and theorists at Rand and other think tanks tried to figure out what kind of new weapons the Russians would have six to eight years from now, in order to fashion American weapons to meet or exceed the challenge.

In testimony before Congress some years ago John S. Foster Jr., director of research and engineering at the Pentagon, put it this way: "We are moving ahead to make sure that, whatever they [the Russians] do, or the possible things *we imagine* they might do, we will be prepared. . . ." (Emphasis added.) Sometimes their guesses were grossly wrong, as for instance when they spent $18 billion on the SAGE continental air defense system because they thought it would "deter" the Russians from improving their bomber fleet; it turned out that the Soviets put a low priority on this project at the time. The scientists and engineers continue with their work, however, and once they come up with a new weapons system—say the neutron bomb—the militarists elaborate a strategical purpose to hatch it. There is never any such thing as "enough."

Second, there evolved a set of powerful constituencies with an immense stake in the arms race. Strongest of all was the Pentagon. One might suppose that in a nuclear age the role of the military should be to avoid war, but the Pentagon argued—with some cogency—that its very existence was a mandate to find a way to *win* wars, and it seized on that goal with unparalleled determination. In the process it built an empire such as the world has never seen—$228 billion of wealth (more than that of the fifteen largest utilities and fifteen largest industrial companies combined), more land than the seven smallest states put together, and thousands of lobbyists and public relations persons to sell the program of "more."

With this outlook and the almost limitless sums at its disposal (the only major weapons system it has been denied since World War II is the B-1 bomber), the Pentagon has been able to feed and fatten a host of other constituencies that help it promote the arms race. They include the big corporations, each one seeking a piece of the $40-odd billion in military procurement; the AFL-CIO leaders who depend on the arms race for jobs for their members; the think tanks and private institutions like the American Security Council, which develop the ideological arguments for continuing the race; parts of the academic community; legislators bidding for military installations for their districts; the media; local officials, and others. Never before in our history has there been so powerful a complex designed to bend the public mind in the militarist direction.

Finally, there is the postwar phenomenon of anti-communism. Early in the cold war, Senate Minority Leader Arthur Vandenberg expressed what has undoubtedly been the prevailing opinion in Washington. If the United States was to spend more money on "preparedness" it was necessary, he said, "to scare the hell out of the country." The government has been doing it ever since, with a raucous brand of anti-communism meant to convince America's citizenry that if it doesn't vote $128 billion military budgets the Russians will overrun us. Without this anti-communism (preached universally in high places, incidentally, not just by the likes of Joe McCarthy) the arms race could never have risen to its present peak.

What we have, then, is an impersonal system in which scientists and engineers develop new horror instruments without letup; a host of constituencies, with a material or ideological stake in militarism, to promote those weapons, and a vulgar type of anti-communism to seduce the public into believing it is necessary. This triad sustains the arms race, and sooner or later will lead us to Doomsday.

It is folly to believe that the arms race can be terminated by the efforts of "good men"—doves like Andrew Young or Paul Warnke, for instance. Lacking a strong public demand for disarmament, the area within which "good men" must work is narrow. At best, they can slow the *rate of escalation*. They can honestly argue that if they stray too far toward a consistent anti-militarist position they will either be removed from their posts or defeated in elections. What is needed is an aroused populace, building the pressures as in the Vietnam days outside the cloister of government—but ultimately affecting it.

It is not an insurmountable task, and the forces to lead it are currently being assembled. But it will not happen through spontaneous combustion or at no cost. The present generation will have to bestir itself, just as the last generation did against the war in Vietnam—only much more so. For in the truest sense of the word, survival itself depends on it.

REMEMBRANCES OF THINGS PAST[4]

As America debates whether to ratify the new SALT agreement, it is useful to recall what happened in the first great period of arms limitation agreements, 1921–1936. A brief look at the details of the Washington Naval Treaty of 1922, the most successful of the interwar negotiations, sheds some light on current questions.

Unlike SALT I and II, the Washington treaty involved serious arms *reduction:* Each of the three main naval pow-

[4] From article entitled "An Earlier Attempt to Limit Arms," by Charles H. Fairbanks Jr., professor of political science at Yale and research director of the Arms Races and Arms Control Project of the Twentieth Century Fund. *Wall Street Journal.* 143:26. Je. 21, '79. Reprinted with permission of the *Wall Street Journal* © 1979 Dow Jones & Company, Inc. All Rights Reserved.

ers scrapped roughly half their existing battleships and almost all of the enormous tonnage under construction. It was agreed that for a decade no new battleships would be built. The core of the treaty was a ratio freezing approximately the strength in battleships then existing, and extending it to aircraft carriers: The ratio among the United States, Britain, and Japan was 5:5:3.

Qualitative limits were imposed as well, limiting battleships to 35,000 tons and cruisers to 10,000 tons (with 8-inch guns). In the London Treaty of 1930 limits were placed on the numbers of other types of ships.

The Washington treaty had real accomplishments. It saved all the countries involved a vast amount of money and stopped for nearly 20 years the increase in battleship size, just then swelling monstrously. The treaty also showed that in circumstances like these, where there was no deep opposition of political interests, stopping an arms race could indeed decrease international tension. Finally, the treaty provided a universal and principled covering which psychologically eased acceptance of shifts in power relationships—Britain's loss of naval superiority for the first time in 200 years and the abandonment of the Anglo-Japanese alliance—that could have been far more disturbing if baldly presented.

At the same time, the treaty turned out not to be, as Lord Balfour, the head of the British delegation, proclaimed, an "absolute unmixed benefit to mankind, which carried no seeds of future misfortune."

To begin with, it soon became apparent that the treaty had actually spurred the arms race in important ways. Stephen Roskill, the naval historian, writes that "all in all, the first effect of the limitation treaty on Britain . . . was to produce greater activity in naval building than at any time since the armistice [of 1918]." No one foresaw this outcome, but it is hardly surprising. To negotiate, a nation needs to carefully compare its forces with those of other countries, highlighting areas of relative weakness. Then, in order to reassure doubters about the treaty, these missing forces must be supplied, as President Carter proposes to do with the MX. It is thus all too easy for the arms limitation process to wind up in incessant arms accumulation to remedy security weaknesses created or brought to light by the original agreements: the equivalent of pouring water into a perforated bucket.

A New Weapon

As soon as the battleship race was halted in the early twenties, a race began in cruisers, which had been relatively neglected. The United States had only three modern cruisers, the British Empire 60. The cruisers constructed after the treaty displaced 10,000 tons, the treaty limit, while almost all existing cruisers were half this size and armed with 6-inch or 4-inch guns rather than 8-inch. The arms limitation treaty had quickly brought into existence a new and much more powerful weapon, the "Treaty Cruiser."

It is easy to see why this was likely to take place. The pace of technological innovation in weapons is normally limited by the fact that military staffs, like all bureaucracies, are embedded in a mass of routine administrative duties. From these ordinary duties there are most likely to emerge conservative, incremental decisions on weapons: Adding a few, or improving the type slightly, with each budget cycle.

A treaty negotiation, on the other hand, forces far-reaching reassessment of weapons policy. To develop their negotiating positions, the American, British, and Japanese governments needed to know from their naval staffs what was the most useful type of cruiser. It is scarcely surprising that the answer turned out to be that the optimum cruiser is a cruiser twice as big as existing cruisers.

By a somewhat similar process the Washington treaty

encouraged the emergence of the aircraft carrier, a new weapon neglected by the battleship admirals then dominating every major navy. In ordinary circumstances those admirals would never have chosen to invest in aircraft carriers rather than battleships. Once their cherished battleship force had been cut to the bone in negotiations, however, they developed a sudden but natural awareness of the need for aircraft carriers, and discovered that the unfinished hulls of four battleships just stricken under the treaty terms could be converted quite nicely into giant aircraft carriers for the U.S. and Japan.

In two crucial areas, then, the Washington treaty's effort to reduce weapons actually resulted in more weapons and in faster technological development of weapons. The general problem posed by these cases is whether there is any way of preventing such unintended consequences, tied to the negotiating process, from countering the intended arms control results of an agreement. If not, we may be forced to ask whether the arms control *treaty* is a bad means of arms control.

There appeared a second problem as well. As Pearl Harbor made clear, the aircraft carrier was a weapon that, as compared with the battleship, encouraged striking first in a crisis, and therefore somewhat increased the chances of war. The aircraft carrier was far better adapted to carry out swift attack from a distance than the lumbering battleship, while at the same time its thin, gasoline-laden hull could not withstand attack like the battleship's thick carapace.

At Midway and other carrier battles there was a strong tendency for the side that struck first to win. If one wants to do everything that would make war less likely—the primary object of all arms limitation agreements—one will not want to encourage the shifting of the weapons mix towards weapons, like the aircraft carrier, that may encourage a first strike. But the Washington treaty had precisely this effect.

Fortifications—a "weapon" that impedes successful war —were prohibited by the treaty in the Western Pacific. This destabilizing concession had to be made to get Japan to accept the politically disagreeable 5:5:3 ratio. The general spirit that dominated arms limitation efforts in the twenties as in SALT II—the opposition to greater quantities of weapons in the abstract—completely blinded negotiators and planners to the particular effects of specific weapons on the preservation of peace.

Looking back at the twenties, it is not clear whether it was the quantity of weapons in the abstract or the character of specific weapons that held out greater danger of war. In the nuclear age, it seems increasingly clear that any danger of the former kind is outweighed by the destabilizing effect of particular weapons, such as big land-based ballistic missiles like the Soviet SS-18, that can annihilate enemy forces when striking first but are vulnerable themselves to attack.

While the treaty worked in some ways to decrease the chances of war and in other ways to increase it, some of its indirect effects weakened U.S. and British security if war did come.

Public opinion in the United States and Britain tended to be lulled by the treaty into ignoring defense. In ten of the 18 years between the treaty and World War II the U.S. Congress did not authorize the building of a single warship, while Japan laid down several ships every year. The result was that by the late thirties Japan, entitled by the 1922 and 1930 treaties to 60% of U.S. strength, had actually been allowed to build to 80% of parity. It proved impossible to restore the treaty ratio by December 7, 1941. As with any commodity where there was zero demand for ten years, the armor plate and heavy gun industries withered, factories were abandoned and workers were retrained in other trades.

When freed of the treaty limits by Japanese abrogation (as of 1936) the U.S. and Britain continued to build

35,000-ton battleships with 14-inch or 16-inch guns, while Japan went immediately to 64,000 tons and 18-inch guns.

As this suggests, the signatories had different conceptions of what the treaty meant. The United States and Britain tended to see their commitment to the treaty as commitment to the spirit of the treaty, which might call for more than its formal provisions. Japan quite honorably interpreted the treaty to mean the letter of the treaty. To get around treaty limits, Japan laid down submarine tenders that could be quickly converted into aircraft carriers and cruisers whose 6-inch guns could be quickly exchanged for the 8-inch guns of heavy cruisers.

The United States also exploited the treaty provisions in less startling ways. By a somewhat sophistic interpretation of an apparently unrelated clause in the Washington treaty American officials squeezed out another 3,000 tons displacement for their new aircraft carriers, but then nervously did not list it in official tables.

New Uncertainty

These cases bring us to a further unintended consequence which the Washington and London treaties share with other arms limitation agreements: They encourage attempts to extract from the treaty unforeseen advantage for one side, and at the extreme, cheating. Deception is always an attractive possibility in arms races, but the need to work within the definite limits imposed by a formal agreement vastly increases the incentives for deception or for testing the limits of the treaty as the U.S. did. This sort of behavior creates in turn new uncertainty, which it is precisely one of the greatest aims of arms limitation agreements to avoid.

The end of the Washington-London treaty system was clear in 1934 when Japan gave the required two years' warning to abrogate the treaty. It is little reproach to an arms limitation treaty that it could not dam up the volcanic forces that had begun to stir and crackle in the Japan of the thirties. But this case does point out a final problem that all arms limitation agreements must face. Arms limitation agreements, which by their very nature involve precise ratios and numbers of arms permitted to each side, are far more specific and detailed than most treaties.

They thus lack the flexibility that enables most international agreements to bend with change and be infused with a new political content—as the meaning of NATO, for example, has shifted substantially over the years. When the rigid structure of an arms limitation agreement can no longer contain changed political forces, it will snap apart. The cost may be heavy: After an arms limitation treaty not renewed, as after a divorce, one cannot return to the starting point.

In the case of the Washington-London treaty system, by the middle thirties Japan had experienced a vast economic and technological growth relative to Britain and the United States; Japan was on the march, while the United States and Britain had become more passive in foreign policy. The naval ratio 5:5:3 inevitably presented itself to many Japanese as the symbol of an inferior position in the international community that no longer corresponded to realities. At the same time the United States and Britain were understandably unwilling to change a ratio that they felt had been definitely nailed down in 1922. The outcome was the 1936 abrogation of a treaty that had already for several years bred in Japan resentment rather than harmony.

Arms control agreements are a means to bring about one of the loftiest human aims, the preservation of peace. By a natural process we have seen the tool as a thing as noble as its purpose. But over the last 58 years of arms limitations agreements it has appeared that this tool has some inherent tendencies to defeat the purpose for which we are using it. From such treaties there have repeatedly emerged major unintended side effects that did not help or, at worst, directly opposed the preservation of peace.

Some specific arms limitation agreements are good on

balance, as the Washington treaty may have been. But the architects of an arms limitation treaty in the 1970s have a duty to explain how they have fashioned its specific provisions to deal with the kinds of unintended consequences that have come to light since the twenties.

II. IN FAVOR OF SALT II

EDITOR'S INTRODUCTION

The success of the SALT I agreements concluded in 1972—if indeed history will judge them a success—has been mainly attributed to the halt they imposed on the costly construction of anti-ballistics missile (ABM) defense systems and missile launchers. However, SALT I did not attempt to halt or reduce strategic advances in offensive nuclear weapons, and it is this category of armament that is the main concern of SALT II. The crucial question is, "Can the U.S. risk limiting its offensive nuclear capabilities in a world where the Soviet regime seeks every tactical and strategic advantage to press its struggle for global supremacy?" The answer, as provided by five articles in this section, is "yes."

The first article, by a State Department expert, Leslie Gelb, brings us up to date with a description and analysis of the terms and conditions of SALT II and its probable effects. The article that follows is by the director of the U.S. Arms Control and Disarmament Agency, Paul C. Warnke, who describes the course of U.S.-Soviet relations from its initial point of unrestricted accumulation of nuclear might to the beginning of control in SALT I, and now to the prospect for quantitative and qualitative restrictions as embodied in SALT II. It is, he argues, a process "we can pursue . . . without risk and, indeed, with major benefit to our national security. SALT, in fact, complements our assured retaliatory capability with less cost and at less risk."

Next, a writer in *Foreign Affairs*, provides a systematic analysis of SALT II's effect on American security and concludes, like Warnke, that our security will be enhanced by its acceptance and that the agreement "sets important and positive precedents for a continuation of the SALT process." In the fourth article, the editors of the *New Republic* favor the ratification of SALT II, arguing that "the Senate should not defeat SALT because the Soviets are up to no good. It is *because* they are up to no good that we need SALT—to insure that we know what they are doing in the most dangerous area of our relationship."

In the fifth article, a Catholic scholar, choosing a middle stance, maintains that SALT II is worth supporting as a start because of its limited but substantial achievements and its promise of a larger vision.

THE FACTS OF SALT II[1]

There are three things you should not expect from SALT.

First, SALT will *not* reduce current defense expenditures. It *will* enable us to spend less than we would in the absence of an agreement. *With* a SALT agreement, expenditures on strategic nuclear forces are likely to rise from 20 to 40% in the coming years; *without* SALT, the same expenditures would rise 50 to 60%.

Second, SALT is *not* going to propel the United States out in front of the Soviet Union in the strategic arms race nor is it going to allow the Russians to gain advantage over us. It *will* allow us to maintain nuclear parity.

Third, SALT will *not* bring on the millennium in U.S.-Soviet relations. SALT *will* be a way to moderate and stabilize these difficult relations, a kind of safety net for what will otherwise be a substantially competitive relationship.

Let me now expand on what we can expect from SALT.

[1] From address before the San Diego World Affairs Council, by Leslie H. Gelb, Director of the Bureau of Politico-Military Affairs, U.S. State Department. *Department of State Bulletin.* 79:24–7. Je. '79.

What Is In the Agreement

First, the SALT II agreement provides for an equal ceiling on strategic delivery vehicles. Each side will be allowed 2,250 delivery vehicles—that is, long-range bombers, land-based ballistic missiles of intercontinental range (ICBM's), and ballistic missiles fired by submarines (SLBM's). This equal ceiling will correct a major problem we had with SALT I, namely, perceptions.

Under SALT I, the Soviet Union was allowed over 2,300 missiles, the United States just a little over 1,700. SALT I thus created a "perception" of Soviet superiority, even though the superiority was not real.

SALT II wipes that away. It forces the Soviets to destroy some 250 existing missiles and/or long-range bombers. Because the United States has only slightly over 2,000 delivery vehicles at this time, we could build up to the 2,250 ceiling, if we so choose.

SALT II will also place limits on the number of warheads. The 2,250 limit refers only to the platforms and launchers on which warheads are placed. The United States now has almost 10,000 nuclear warheads on the launchers limited by SALT. The Soviet Union has nearly 5,000. Within the SALT II limits on warheads, we will still be ahead of the Soviets in the number of warheads by the end of the period covered by this agreement—1985—but the comparative totals will be closer.

The destructive capability of a single Poseidon submarine illustrates the dimensions of nuclear power, the significance of numbers of warheads. Each Poseidon submarine can hit up to 160 separate targets with individual warheads. Each of these warheads has almost three times the destructive power of the bomb dropped on Hiroshima.

The second point about SALT II is that for the first time there will be qualitative controls on technology, on modernization. Part of these qualitative limits are the warhead limits mentioned above. There are specific limits on the number of warheads that can be placed on all SLBM's, on existing ICBM's, and on the one new type of ICBM each side will be permitted until 1985.

That limitation to only one new type of ICBM is, itself, a most significant qualitative control. To insure that it has real meaning, the modernization of existing ICBM's will be limited so that neither side can circumvent the limitation to one new ICBM. There will also be other qualitative limitations which are designed to slow the strategic competition.

Third, we believe we can adequately verify this agreement by our photoreconnaissance satellites and through other national technical means. Thus, the agreement does not depend on believing the Russians but on our own capability to see and estimate that they are complying with the agreement.

That doesn't mean that we can verify each of the many provisions of the agreement with the same degree of confidence. We cannot. Most of the provisions can be verified with good or high confidence. In the case of a few provisions, the confidence is less. However, we believe that we can deal with these particular provisions, even in a "worst case" where the Russians cheated.

On balance, we feel that verification is adequate and that we can deal effectively with the consequences of violation.

Under the SALT I and antiballistic missile (ABM) agreements, it is fair to say that the Soviets pushed the interpretation of many of the provisions to the limit. But on every single occasion—and I underline every—where we drew Soviet attention to a compliance issue, they ended up in compliance with the agreement. Either we cleared up a misunderstanding or they changed their practices.

Fourth, SALT II allows us to continue our patterns of military cooperation with our allies, particularly our NATO allies. This point should be stressed, because one of the most serious pieces of misinformation about SALT is that the agreement will somehow prevent us from continuing to help our allies develop their forces. This is simply nonsense. As Secretary [of Defense Harold H.] Brown and senior military officers have testified to Congress, this agreement does not hamper our ability to continue those patterns of cooperation, including helping our allies modernize their forces.

Finally, the agreement allows the United States to go forward with every single strategic nuclear program now on our drawing boards—every one of them. The SALT agreement does not slow down our plans to develop the cruise missile. It does not in any way impair our ability to move forward with new programs for SLBM's—Trident I and Trident II—with the new Trident submarine, or the new M–X land-based missile. Our military options are open.

All this being said about the terms of the agreement, what does it add up to in arms control value? What is being controlled? The honest answer is that the agreement has us taking a step toward control, toward limitation, rather than just accepting unrestrained competition and all that that entails. This is not an insignificant statement —it is a major statement.

In politics, people often scoff at moving on the margins, moving a little here, moving a little there. It's not enough; it doesn't amount to a hill of beans, so some say. Why are we paying such a high price for so little? One really has to understand what arms control is all about to understand why this agreement is so important. Arms control is, in its essence, a confidence-building exercise.

What if we didn't have SALT II? Even with the agreement, we will do what is necessary to compete with the Soviets. No responsible political leader would choose otherwise. That is not the issue. The issue is that, if we both decided to increase our spending substantially on strategic forces, we would end up with a lot more bucks having been spent and no more security. In the nuclear age absolute security is no longer in the cards. Part of our growing up and learning to live with this situation is understanding that fact.

The Treaty and the U.S.-Soviet Strategic Balance

How then does this agreement fit into the general Soviet-American nuclear balance? The first point is that we are strong, that we are not getting weaker, that we are getting stronger. We have underway the nuclear programs that I have mentioned and others, as well as programs to modernize our conventional forces. We are not sitting on our laurels and taking chances with our security. I am very discouraged, as I have gone around the country, to hear so many American political leaders bad-mouthing our military strength, portraying the Soviets as 10 feet tall and the United States as a midget. The danger is that the Soviets and others might believe this and act on it, even though it is not true.

Let me now address a subject that has gained considerable attention and that will continue to be discussed throughout the SALT debate. It is called "ICBM vulnerability," and it lies at the heart of judgments being made about the future of the strategic balance.

As missiles become more accurate, they have more capability to destroy other missiles which are still in silos waiting to be launched. So a situation is evolving where our ICBM force—the Minuteman force—will in the early 1980s become vulnerable in theory to a Soviet first-strike. This is of concern to many people both inside and outside the Administration. If we keep the problem in perspective, we realize that we cannot be relaxed about it, but neither do we have to panic or react hastily with quick fixes and short-term solutions.

Based on our projections of what the Soviet force will be capable of in the early 1980s we now estimate that they will have the theoretical capability to destroy up to 90% of our 1,000 Minuteman missiles in a surprise first-strike.

But this is a "worst case" scenario and one which I believe the Soviets could never count upon in making their strategic plans. Let me outline some of the assumptions they would have to make to act upon this situation of ICBM vulnerability.

—The Soviets would have to assume optimum performance by their missile force in a first-strike, including complete surprise. But no one has ever planned, coordinated, and launched such an attack. The imponderables are numerous and enormous. The effects of "fratricide," for example, where incoming missiles destroy each other, are and will remain big question marks.

—They would have to assume we would leave our ICBM's in the silos and let them be destroyed; that is, that we would not launch these ICBM's even though we knew a Soviet *attack* was under way. But they would be taking great risks to make such an assumption. And if we launch under attack, their missiles would blow up empty silos. The exchange would cripple the Soviet strategic forces and would still leave the United States with its submarines and bombers relatively untouched (and these remaining forces represent between two-thirds to three-fourths of our nuclear strike force). But that's not all.

—The Soviets would have to assume that we would be so paralyzed by their strike that we would not respond with our remaining ICBM's and all of our submarines and bombers against Soviet cities for fear of inviting Soviet attack against U.S. cities. But if the Soviets struck to destroy all of our ICBM's somewhere between 8 and 20 million Americans would be killed virtually right away. The Soviets would be fools to launch an attack on the assumption that we would not strike back. I said they are not supermen; they are not fools either.

What I am saying is that the real-world danger will be much less than what the doomsayers are predicting. This danger to our ICBM force, however, has not yet arrived, and since we see it coming we are working to correct it.

One of the main options being considered to solve this problem—the mobile land-based missile—would not be feasible without SALT. SALT didn't create the problem of Minuteman vulnerability. The problem results from the increasing accuracy and destructive power of new Soviet missiles. But, paradoxically, only SALT can make the land-based mobile missile idea a viable one, because it limits the number of warheads that can be placed on ICBM's. Without SALT, the Soviets could just keep putting more warheads on their missiles every time we build a new hole in the ground to hide our missiles.

In sum, SALT does not hurt the strategic balance and U.S. long-term security; it enhances it. This Administration is working, as its predecessors have worked, to keep the United States secure. The weapons programs planned or underway will do just that through the period of SALT II and beyond. We can do the job without SALT, but we can do the job much better with SALT.

SALT and U.S.-Soviet Relations

Even if we have a sense of confidence about future security, about measures we are taking to deal with it, how does SALT affect the broader picture of U.S.-Soviet relations? There are two general concerns. One is: Why do we want to have an agreement like this with the Russians when they are acting as they are in Africa or Iran or Indochina? Why don't we withhold SALT until they behave themselves in these other parts of the world? The other concern is: Isn't SALT fundamentally dangerous to the American body politic and isn't it somehow going to lull the American people into a false sense of security and make them think there is peace when there really isn't?

The question is whether we should tell the Soviets that we won't move forward on SALT unless they cease and desist in the Horn of Africa or Iran or Indochina or elsewhere. To begin with we are not negotiating SALT as a favor to the Russians, a favor we will withdraw if they are not "nice guys" elsewhere. We are signing the SALT agreement because it is in our interest to do so; it makes strategic sense. The Soviet Union is in SALT for the same reasons. If we seek to tie the fate of SALT, and all that hinges on it, to the achievement of some benchmark in U.S.-Soviet relations, or to Soviet acceptance of our interests in other parts of the world, it will not solve these other problems and we will not have SALT either. The Soviets will pursue their interests, attempting to gain influence elsewhere in the world, and so will we. SALT does not mean the competition is over everywhere, just that the strategic competition, because of mutual interests, will be limited to some degree.

By the same token, going ahead with SALT does not mean we are caving in to the Soviets elsewhere either. We can bring our resources to bear on Soviet behavior in the Third World. We do that, but it is not easy—just as it is not easy for the Soviets simply to accept our stepping in where they have had difficulties or failed such as in Egypt, the Arab-Israel negotiations, Indonesia, Sudan, and elsewhere.

The other concern is that SALT is somehow putting the American people to sleep, leading them to think that "détente" solves all our problems and that the Soviets are our trusted friends. The policy of this Administration—and previous ones as well—is to develop some elements of cooperation even as we compete with the Soviets. It's a mixed, complicated, and even inconsistent relationship, but that's life. It's the kind of thing people accept as normal in dealing with other people. A mature relationship, even with an adversary, necessitates building some bridges of restraint and moderation at the same time as we compete and challenge. It's hard to get some critics to accept this in foreign policy, even though it is readily accepted in their private lives and business relationships. As I move around the country, I am concerned, from what I hear, that the critics are creating a climate where there is less and less willingness to tolerate this type of commonsense, mixed relationship with the Soviet Union.

In the late 1970s there is less tolerance for complexities. I am concerned that this kind of attitude is affecting how we come to terms with something like SALT, which I think lies at the very heart of a sensible, but complex, foreign policy. What is required here is a steadiness, a sense of balance, an awareness of risks and opportunities, and a maturity. In the end, what we are trying to do, what we are trying to persuade you to believe, is that SALT is a part of a process, part of a hard-nosed, pragmatic, American way of attempting to deal with our security. SALT is not a substitute for a strong national defense. It is, in our judgment, a necessary supplement to it.

SALT II: WHAT IT MEANS, WHAT IT DOES[2]

. . . What I would like to do . . . is to ask you to step back and take a long view of SALT, as a process, to consider how and why we became involved in it, what we have accomplished to date, and what we have come to learn of the implications of SALT—first and foremost for our national security, but also for our relations with the Soviet Union—because SALT deals with the core of the power balance between the United States and the Soviet Union, specifically with the most important and most dangerous component of that balance, those nuclear weapons which, if ever used, would mean the devastation of both societies.

So SALT thus involves fundamental and vital security interests of both countries. Because this is so, you might ask why the SALT talks didn't begin until the late 1960s.

[2] From an address before the Foreign Policy Association, "SALT Two—The Home Stretch," by Paul C. Warnke, Director, Arms Control and Disarmament Agency. August 23, 1978. *Department of State Bulletin.* 78:17-23. O. '78.

Why was it that they didn't start sooner—perhaps in the early 1950s?

Background of SALT

I think the answer to this question can be found in the history of U.S.-Soviet relations and the evolution of the military balance between these countries since the end of World War II and the beginning of the nuclear age. Out of the wartime alliance, and with Europe and Japan in ruins, the United States and the Soviet Union emerged as the two dominant and rival powers.

Fundamental differences in goals, values, and political systems led inevitably to this rivalry and to a bipolar world. And for many years any kind of useful relations or productive negotiations between our two countries appeared almost impossible. Many questioned whether we could even live together, and the term "coexistence" acquired a pejorative connotation. So that arms control in these circumstances seemed a very unpromising prospect.

Moreover, you have to remember that for about two decades we had, first, a nuclear monopoly and then a clear nuclear superiority. For the Soviet Union, arms control negotiations—in the light of this great American lead—seemed to offer nothing but permanent second class status. And for the United States, because of our immensely greater strategic capability, arms control was a topic of no particular urgency.

The Soviets could not be expected to allow this lead to persist as long as they possessed the resources to close the gap. Even if our strategic nuclear edge did not allow us consistently to thwart Soviet foreign policy objectives and its ability to project its military power, a combination of historic Russian sensitivity to the activities of the West and Soviet ideology drive the U.S.S.R., at no small cost, to try and catch up with the United States in strategic nuclear forces.

By the mid-1960s, programs for this Soviet effort were

firmly established and underway, and thus the two super-powers were forced to face the implications of the new military reality. For the United States, it meant that no longer could we rely—either in practice or even in rhetoric —on the doctrine of massive nuclear retaliation, a doctrine that actually had been eroding for nearly a decade.

Since the late 1950s, it has become increasingly clear that Soviet possession of a nuclear retaliatory capability meant instead that our military forces must be capable of flexible response, commensurate with the military challenge; because otherwise the Soviet Union would be left with wide freedom of action to use, or threaten to use, its conventional military power.

Now there have been some who have argued that we never should have allowed the Russians to overcome our nuclear superiority. A group recently formed insists that we should now regain that strategic nuclear superiority. They do not, however, tell us how that can be done; nor do they say how the effort to do so can be kept from creating an unbridled competition and the accumulation of further and more deadly nuclear weapons that would mean superiority for neither side and diminished security for both.

The fact is that in a nuclear race between countries with the resources of the United States and the Soviet Union, one side can gain and maintain strategic superiority only if the other side defaults. Now we know that we would never be willing to concede nuclear superiority to the Soviets, and I think we have no basis for hoping that they may be more indulgent and give us that advantage.

So it is the inescapable logic of strategic nuclear weapons and the terrible consequences of their wide-scale use, if strategic stability should disappear and deterrence should fail, that even bitter competitors have to give serious thought to the benefits of limited cooperation in the form of arms control. This is the case for us, whatever our distaste for Soviet ambitions abroad and repression at home.

You will remember that the first manifestation of this dawning realism about nuclear arms came in the consideration of the deployment of antiballistic missile systems. In the mid-1960s, the Soviets were expanding their air defense and beginning to deploy some ballistic missile defenses, and the question we had to face was whether we should move our research and development program on antiballistic missiles beyond that development stage into actual deployment, and there were those within government who consistently urged that course.

McNamara Legacy

What I regard as the seminal statement in the new strategic arms debate was a speech delivered by the then-Secretary of Defense, Robert McNamara, in 1967. This was an historic contribution to public understanding of strategic policy.

In his speech, Secretary McNamara outlined the basic concepts of nuclear strategy and explained the new realities of deterrence and the mutual vulnerability of the United States and the Soviet Union to the ballistic missiles of the other side. He emphasized that the problem with ABMs, with antiballistic missile defenses, was not the problem of cost, but the fact that the system itself was vulnerable to countermeasures which the other side could take. No matter how many antiballistic missiles one side might assemble, the other side could match that, and more than match that, with offensive nuclear warheads and also with dummy warheads.

So that even if the ABM were technically feasible, United States deployment of a massive anti-Soviet ABM system would, as Secretary McNamara put it, have "strongly motivated [the Soviets] to so increase their offensive capability as to cancel out our defensive advantages."

We could, as the Secretary of Defense pointed out, guess at Soviet intentions, match their ABM deployments, respond to internal pressures for new offensive systems to overcome the antiballistic missile defenses, and try to preserve our security interests in a new round of the nuclear arms race. "But," he continued, "what we would much prefer to do is to come to a realistic and reasonably riskless agreement with the Soviet Union, which would effectively prevent such an arms race."

And with that speech, Mr. McNamara placed negotiated arms control explicitly where it belongs—in the context of national security.

It was really out of this new perception of the strategic realities that SALT was born. It was the relative parity of the strategic nuclear forces of both sides that made SALT possible, and it was the stability of that balance that made SALT desirable.

When the United States was still strategically superior, the Soviet Union didn't dare to negotiate, and we felt no need to do so. But once parity was achieved, another round of the arms race with the rich, strong-willed, and technologically powerful United States would provide the Soviet Union with neither greater security nor greater status; because with the forces in relative balance, neither side could rationally be tempted to launch a preemptive first strike.

President Johnson, in tying his actions on ABMs to Soviet willingness to negotiate limitations on ABMs, was really the one who committed the United States to the SALT process. And every President since then, Republican and Democratic, has continued that commitment to arms control.

Their consistent belief is expressed in President Carter's introduction to my agency's 1977 annual report. He noted that, "when necessary, we will maintain our security and protect our interests by strengthening our military capabilities. Whenever possible, however, we seek to enhance our security through arms control. Our security, and the security of all nations, can be better served through equitable and verifiable limits on arms than through unbridled competition. The United States has chosen arms control as an essential means of promoting its security."

Meaning of SALT I

In SALT there already have been significant accomplishments. The SALT ONE agreements in 1972 included a treaty which drastically limited anti-ballistic missile defenses, and that treaty was so successful that it was later amended to cut back the permitted deployment of ABM systems from two to one. The ABM Treaty logically removed a major incentive to build up offensive systems; because of the fact that the ABMs were essentially banned, it meant that you did not have to engage in a further accumulation of offensive warheads in order to penetrate what would become a non-existent defense.

In addition, in SALT ONE, there was an interim agreement on control of strategic offensive arms. This essentially froze the number of strategic missile launchers at the levels already deployed or under construction.

Taken together, these SALT ONE agreements constituted recognition that the key to strategic stability and to a lower risk of nuclear war was to preserve the retaliatory capability of each side; and that, accordingly, building of more and more offensive weapons was unnecessary, dangerous, and inconsistent with our goal of a secure world.

Since May of 1972, when SALT ONE was signed in Moscow, the careful and at times, I would say, painful development of a SALT TWO agreement has been proceeding. In late 1974, there was a major breakthrough. President Ford and the then General Secretary Brezhnev agreed in Vladivostok that the SALT TWO agreement would provide for equal aggregates in intercontinental nuclear delivery systems.

Moreover, the Soviet side agreed that these equal numbers could be part of the new treaty, without any compensation to them for the fact that the United States maintains—in bases in Europe—the so-called "forward-based systems" that enable us to target additional thousands of nuclear weapons against the Soviet Union.

It is important that we now embody this principle of equal aggregates in a formal treaty, because even if it were limited to this feature alone, SALT TWO would be very much in the interests of the United States. And from this starting point of equal ceilings on the number of total launchers, and launchers of missiles with multiple, independently-targetable reentry vehicles that we refer to as MIRVs, we can go on to parallel reductions in these ceilings. It has already been agreed at Geneva that Vladivostok ceilings of 2,400 strategic nuclear-delivery vehicles, of which 1,320 can be MIRVed, will be cut back early on in the course of SALT TWO. And it has also been agreed that there will be a separate subceiling on the land-based intercontinental ballistic missiles with MIRVs.

We want that separate sub-ceiling, because these are the most dangerous, the most destabilizing of the nuclear weapons. They are the ones that pose the greater threat of a counterforce capability against the missile forces of the other side, and hence a threat to the assured retaliatory capability.

Lessons from Negotiation

As we have moved in the last decade of SALT from unrestricted accumulation of nuclear weapons to the beginning of control, and now to the prospect of effective quantitative as well as qualitative restrictions, we have learned a good deal about the process. We have learned a good deal about how it works and what it means for the U.S.-Soviet relationship.

The first lesson that we have learned is that we can negotiate about strategic arms, and that the resulting agreements will work. The Antiballistic Missile Limitation Treaty did, in fact, limit the deployment of ballistic missile defenses. I pointed out that we have cut back from two sites in each country to one; and, as a matter of fact, we have deactivated our own one site, because we don't need it to protect our deterrent.

The second lesson is that strategic arms control agreements can be developed which are, in fact, verifiable by our national technical means. Unless we can have adequate assurance that the other side is complying with arms control provisions, any arms control agreement will become a source of suspicion and friction, rather than a source of comfort and confidence. With our highly sophisticated national technical means of verification, we don't have to rely on Soviet assurances. We have been able to determine, under the SALT ONE agreements, and we will be able to determine, under a SALT TWO agreement, that the limits, both quantitative and qualitative, are, in fact, being met by the Soviet Union.

The provisions on verification that have already been agreed upon prohibit any measures of deliberate concealment which would impede our ability to verify compliance, and they specifically prohibit any interference with our national technical means. Moreover, after long negotiation, and in the fact of the traditional Soviet reluctance to disclose facts on military forces, the Soviet negotiators agreed earlier this year to an exchange of data that will establish an agreed data base against which we can measure the reductions to the new agreed-upon lower ceilings.

And because of the impossibility of determining by national technical means what kind of a missile is in any particular missile launcher, we have now agreed that a launcher will be counted as a launcher of a MIRV missile if it is of a type which has ever contained or launched a missile which is of a type which has ever been tested with MIRVs. That supplements our national technical means of verification and gives us an identifiable feature against which we can measure compliance with the SALT ceilings.

There is a third, and I think a very important, lesson

that we have learned in the SALT process, and that's the fact that arms control agreements only limit those things that are specifically covered by the agreement. We can't rely on compliance with the spirit of an agreement; you have to have the letter. You have to have something to which you can point and say that this is an agreed-upon provision which limits the activity in which each side can engage. And we have to recognize that any new weapon, or any new development, that is excluded from the coverage of the agreement is permitted for both sides—that to the extent that we preserve options, we preserve them also for the Soviet Union.

For example, the SALT ONE agreement limited antiballistic missiles, and it limited launchers of offensive missiles of intercontinental range. It didn't limit warheads, and it didn't limit MIRV testing and MIRV deployment. So it is somewhat ironical that although SALT ONE banned any major deployment of antiballistic missiles, because these would lead to offensive countermeasures such as MIRVs, SALT ONE left MIRVs to run free.

Now, today, in the course of the development of SALT TWO, a frequent criticism that I hear is that SALT TWO won't prevent the Soviets from acquiring the theoretical potential to threaten land-based forces in a counterforce first strike.

I have mentioned that intercontinental ballistic missiles with MIRVs are the most dangerous, the most destabilizing of nuclear weapons systems, because they possess the combination of accuracy and yield that enables them to strike hard targets, such as our hardened Minuteman silos. Now, without SALT, this possible vulnerability would obviously become greater, but the threat, at least in theory, does exist. It exists because of the fact that the Soviets have been able to multiply their warheads, because SALT ONE did not prevent the development of MIRVs.

So the MIRV option that we chose to keep open for ourselves has thus come back to haunt us. Now, in SALT

TWO, the reductions in MIRV ballistic missile launchers—
and particularly the sub-ceiling that I have mentioned on
MIRVed intercontinental ballistic missiles—will make a
beginning toward meeting this problem; but it won't be
until SALT THREE, at the earliest, that we will be able
fully to undo that which SALT ONE allowed to be done
in proliferating reentry vehicles.

I would say then that the third lesson we have learned
from SALT is that in the SALT process we should protect
only those military options we genuinely need and those in
which the net balance, if both sides go ahead, will at least
be equal, and preferably, will give us some benefits.

We should avoid those things which mean only an unnecessary and futile intensification of the nuclear arms
competition. And it is with this thought in mind that we
arrived at a three-piece framework for SALT TWO.

Provisions of SALT II

SALT TWO will consist of three parts. One is the basic
agreement, which, as it now stands in the Joint Draft text,
places specific limits through 1985 on total launchers, on
launchers of MIRV missiles, and on launchers of MIRVed
ICBMs.

The second part is a short-term protocol, which puts
short-term limits on certain types of systems on which we
are not yet ready to make a final program decision. For the
period of the protocol, deployment of mobile launchers of
ICBMs is banned. For that same protocol period, there is a
ban on the actual deployment of long-range ground and
sea-launched cruise missiles. The testing of these systems
can continue; and while the protocol continues, we can
determine whether longer-term restrictions should be negotiated as part of SALT THREE, or whether our interests
warrant the actual production and deployment of these new
systems.

We will, of course, have to keep in mind the experience
of the matching Soviet development of MIRVs and be alert

to the fact that if we elect to have the freedom to go ahead with these new systems after the period of the protocol, we must anticipate that the Soviets will do the same. The desirability of preserving the options must be balanced against the possibly adverse effects of the introduction of a new nuclear weapons system into the strategic arms competition.

There is a fourth lesson that has been taught us during a decade of SALT and that is that in the context of overall U.S.-Soviet relations, SALT has developed a value and a momentum of its own. Since 1969, the common recognition that we share an interest in survival has enabled SALT to continue despite the intermittent strains in the U.S.-Soviet relationship.

I mentioned earlier the many differences between the United States and the Soviet Union. With or without SALT, I think we have to anticipate that we will continue to be competitors who share unmatched military power, but very little else; that we will continue to have very different views of a desirable world order and of a domestic system which promotes the well-being of its citizens. We have to expect that there will be times of tension, times when the international dialogue will be bitter and abrasive. Our disagreement with many Soviet policies and many of its actions, both within and outside the Soviet Union, will necessarily affect our attitude toward that government.

But we pursue SALT to lessen the risk of nuclear war and to insure our own survival as a modern, functioning society. I therefore—and I am sure this will come as no surprise to you—find myself in total disagreement with those who have suggested that we should cancel or suspend the SALT talks because of Soviet and Cuban intervention in Africa, or Soviet suppression of independent voices within that country. As I see it, SALT is not just a byproduct of détente, nor can it be used as a bribe to make the Soviets behave in a fashion of which we approve.

SALT, of course, doesn't exist in total isolation. The

Soviet invasion of Czechoslovakia, almost exactly a decade ago, had the further tragic consequence of postponing for more than a year the initiation of talks on limiting strategic nuclear arms. As indicated in President Johnson's memoirs, he was prepared to announce on August 21, 1968, that he and Premier Kosygin would meet on September 30 to begin strategic arms limitation talks. But it was on August 20 that Soviet, Bulgarian, East German, Hungarian, and Polish army units moved into Czechoslovakia.

Neither American nor international public opinion would have understood the initiation of arms control discussions in the unhealthy climate of the summer that followed the Prague spring. And by that fall, when talks might have been started, the Johnson Administration had run out of time. So, it was not until November 17, 1969—in a new U.S. Administration—that American and Soviet delegations met in Helsinki and exchanged the opening statements on the limitation of strategic arms.

But since then SALT has gone ahead despite many U.S.-Soviet frictions. SALT ONE—we have to remember—was signed in May of 1972, just about a month after the United States had mined Haiphong Harbor and trapped Soviet ships.

We have pursued, and we will continue to pursue, our aims in the field of human rights; but Soviet resentment about this has never caused any ripples in our negotiations in Geneva. The issue has never been raised with me by any Soviet negotiator.

We can't be sure that continued progress in the SALT process will improve détente, but I believe we can be certain if SALT fails, the chances of improved relations and of channeling the U.S.-Soviet rivalry into less dangerous areas of competition would be immeasurably damaged.

To me, the relationship between SALT and détente is much like the relationship between SALT and the goal of halting the proliferation of nuclear weapons. Success in

SALT won't automatically bring either détente or non-proliferation, but the failure of SALT would leave us with a very dismal prospect of achieving either objective.

SALT and Security

There is a fifth lesson that I think is to be learned from our experience with SALT, and that is that we can pursue it without risk and, indeed, with major benefits to our national security. SALT, in fact, complements our assured retaliatory capability with less cost and at less risk.

To begin with, we can proceed with SALT because of the fact that we have the technology, the resources, and the forces to meet our strategic military needs. We are not negotiating from fear, but we are negotiating with confidence. We are negotiating from strength, and not from weakness.

To illustrate my point, a study recently completed by the Arms Control and Disarmament Agency vividly shows that while pursuing SALT, we have maintained the retaliatory capability that protects us against the use, or threatened use, of Soviet nuclear forces. Today, our retaliatory capability could do more damage to the Soviet Union after a Soviet first strike than that first strike could to the United States. Our second strike destructive capability exceeds the Soviet Union's first strike capability.

And our study also shows that while the United States and Soviet forces will both become substantially more capable and, really, essentially equal in capability by the mid-1980s, our retaliatory capability after a Soviet first strike will at that time exceed our current ability to retaliate against Soviet targets.

In a speech . . . delivered [in August 1978], Secretary of Defense Harold Brown confirmed this increase in our second strike capability, despite any improvements in the Soviet offensive or defensive forces. This, I would submit, doesn't square with the image, which is suggested by some, that the United States has been hamstrung by SALT, while the Soviets race ahead.

SALT has left us free to make those changes in each part of our deterrent nuclear triad—the intercontinental ballistic missiles, the submarine launched ballistic missiles, and our heavy bombers—which will ensure their viability in the light of Soviet military improvements.

SALT TWO will enable us to go ahead with the military options which our military planners tell us are necessary. Under the limits of SALT TWO, our heavy bomber force will be modernized by being equipped with long-range cruise missiles, missiles with a range that enables them to stay outside of Soviet air defenses and still strike the lucrative Soviet targets.

We are free to go ahead with the Trident ballistic missile submarine and the longer-range ballistic missiles that can be launched from ocean areas close to the United States, and still maintain complete target coverage of the Soviet Union.

Finally, SALT TWO will impose meaningful limits on Soviet strategic forces. To comply with the agreement, the Soviets will have to dismantle or destroy up to several hundred strategic systems. The new agreement, furthermore, will hold the deployment of Soviet strategic forces well below what they would deploy in the absence of an agreement. Our intelligence sources indicate that the net swing in the number of Soviet strategic nuclear delivery systems targeted against the United States is something in the order of 900—that means 900 less systems as a result of SALT. And that, by any definition, is a plus for American security.

I have suggested that SALT is a process. I don't think that SALT TWO is going to be the ultimate word in strategic arms control. It will mean a meaningful step forward, but we should regard this as a continuing process in which we move deliberately, cautiously, but confidently toward the effective control of strategic nuclear weapons and the

elimination of the greatest threat to the survival of the
United States and of the world.

IN DEFENSE OF AMERICAN SECURITY[3]

A new strategic arms limitation treaty between the
United States and the Soviet Union (SALT II) is now essentially complete. As is always the case with a complicated
negotiation, each side has conditioned acceptance of key
provisions on the successful resolution of remaining open
issues. Thus, it is always possible that the process will break
down as each side plays out its end game. But at this stage,
it seems extremely unlikely that the basic provisions of the
agreement will change further.

The ensuing ratification debate will be one of the major
foreign policy debates of the decade, and one of the most
intellectually challenging. The complexities of nuclear
strategy, weapons technology and our overall policy toward
the Soviet Union all come together in SALT. Some will
evaluate the treaty primarily from a political perspective,
assessing its role in both domestic and international politics; others will focus on predominantly technical questions,
such as the extent to which the treaty actually limits the
nuclear deployments of the two sides. Yet SALT is much
more than either a political exercise or arms control for its
own sake. To be successful, SALT must improve our security by helping to stabilize the strategic balance between
the United States and the Soviet Union. Evaluating strategic stability involves complex technical questions, and
even among the experts there is no consensus on how to
measure the strategic balance. But, in the end, no final judgment on the new treaty's worth can be rendered without

[3] Article entitled "SALT II and American Security," by Jan M. Lodal,
executive vice president of American Management Systems, Inc. *Foreign Affairs.*
57:245–68. Winter '78–9. Reprinted by permission from *Foreign Affairs,* Winter
1978–79. Copyright 1978 by Council on Foreign Relations, Inc.

considering the projected stability of the U.S.-U.S.S.R. strategic relationship during the next decade.

Other considerations, such as the success of our negotiators in obtaining Soviet agreement to our positions, our ability to verify Soviet compliance, and the agreement's effect on our allies are also important in assessing the worth of the new treaty. The following sections contain analyses of the new agreement according to each of these criteria, as well as an evaluation of its likely effect on the strategic balance between the Soviet Union and the United States. I believe these analyses demonstrate that those who examine the technical provisions of the new agreement carefully will find little to criticize. SALT II will undoubtedly stimulate intense debate, but in the end, this debate is likely to focus on the pros and cons of the SALT process itself, rather than those of this particular treaty.

The negotiation of the SALT II treaty . . . has been underway for four years—since President Ford and President Brezhnev agreed on the basic framework at Vladivostok in November 1974. Not surprisingly, a negotiation of this duration has resulted in significant changes and additions to the original agreement.

Vladivostok Agreements

The new treaty's numerical limits provide an illuminating example of these changes. The key result of the Vladivostok negotiations was to limit both strategic nuclear delivery vehicles (the sum of land-based intercontinental-range ballistic missiles [ICBMs], submarine-launched ballistic missiles [SLBMs], long-range air-launched ballistic missiles, and heavy bombers) and MIRVed missiles (missiles equipped with multiple independently targetable reentry vehicles) to equal numbers for each side—2,400 delivery vehicles and 1,320 MIRVed missiles. The Ford Administration received significant criticism of the 2,400 and 1,320 limitations, primarily that they were so high that they represented little real constraint on the programs of either side. Secretary of State Kissinger continued to push the Soviets for lower numbers in subsequent negotiations, and by the time the Carter Administration took office, the Soviets had already agreed to reduce the overall ceiling to a number "below 2,300." They have now accepted a final limit of 2,250 rather than 2,400 on the total number of launchers, and also agreed to reduce the limit on MIRVed missiles from 1,320 to 1,200. A new sub-limit of 820 on land-based MIRVed missiles will also be set.

While these revised limits are not as low as some would like, they do have a significant effect on Soviet programs. The reduction in the overall ceiling to 2,250 will require the Soviets to dismantle an additional 150 older systems, although it will have no effect on U.S. force levels. The limit of 1,200 on MIRV launchers cuts somewhat into the U.S. plan to deploy 1,238 MIRVs by 1985, but it will almost certainly require a greater cutback in the Soviet MIRV program. The new sub-limit of 820 on land-based MIRVs is perhaps the most important of the revised ceilings; when combined with the limitation on reentry vehicles (warheads) discussed below, it sets an overall ceiling on the total number of Soviet land-based warheads. It also sets an important precedent for including special limitations on land-based MIRVs, the most potentially destabilizing components of the two sides' force structures.

One of the most contentious issues in the negotiations has been that of limits on cruise missiles. The two sides have disagreed on cruise missile limits since immediately after the Vladivostok negotiations. The Soviets took the position that air-launched cruise missiles of a range greater than 600 kilometers should count within the 2,400 ceiling, and that testing and deployment of ground-launched and sea-launched cruise missiles with a range of over 600 kilometers should be banned. The U.S. position was that there should be no limits on cruise missiles.

In the agreement finally reached, air-launched cruise

missiles on heavy bombers, which are especially important to the U.S. defense program, are permitted with no limit on their range. The only limits affecting these systems result from the inclusion of aircraft equipped with long-range cruise missiles within the various numerical ceilings specified by the treaty. Such aircraft will have to count as heavy bombers within the 2,250 overall ceiling on strategic nuclear launchers, as well as within a combined ceiling of 1,320 on MIRVed missiles and cruise missile-equipped aircraft. Furthermore, the average number of cruise missiles on the aircraft equipped to carry them is limited to approximately 30.

These limits have the overall effect of permitting the United States to deploy at least 3,000 long-range cruise missiles on strategic aircraft without having to make any offsetting reduction in other strategic forces. Even more cruise missiles could be deployed by reducing the number of MIRVed missiles on a one-for-one basis as each cruise missile carrier is deployed, but it seems unlikely that the United States would desire to deploy more than 3,000 nuclear-armed cruise missiles, each with a 200–400 kiloton warhead, over the next seven years.

The situation with respect to long-range ground-launched and sea-launched cruise missiles is somewhat more complicated. The position of each side on this issue has changed several times in the course of the negotiations. No mention of these systems was made at Vladivostok, or in the subsequent aide mémoire. But as mentioned above, shortly thereafter the Soviets took the position that the deployment of ground-launched and sea-launched cruise missiles should be banned. During the 1975 Helsinki summit meeting between President Ford and President Brezhnev, the Soviets proposed to count only intercontinental-range (greater than 5,500 kilometers) ground-launched cruise missiles. The United States later decided that it preferred a 2,500-kilometer limit, at which point the Soviets returned to their demand for a 600-kilometer limit. Clearly, neither side has been sure even of its own position in these negotiations.

The final agreement includes no limits on these systems in the treaty itself, but a protocol to the treaty prohibits the deployment of all ground-launched and sea-launched cruise missiles with a range greater than 600 kilometers for three years. The United States has no capability to deploy such systems during the next three years, and there are no limits on testing cruise missiles, should we decide it is in our interest to continue developing them for later deployment. Thus, in a technical and legal sense, there is no effective limit on U.S. land-based or sea-based cruise missiles. Nevertheless, as I discuss subsequently, the protocol has significant political implications for both U.S.-European relations and the dynamics of the SALT III negotiations. It will undoubtedly receive considerable attention as the SALT II debate continues.

Limiting Qualitative Improvements

The major U.S. objective of limiting "qualitative" force improvements (improvements in the capabilities of individual delivery vehicles) has also been achieved. The Soviets agreed over three years ago to limit the throw-weight of individual missiles to that of the largest missiles now deployed in each class—about 7,000 pounds for "light" missiles and 15,000 pounds for "heavy" missiles. But, more importantly, limits have now been placed on new types of land-based missiles and on the number of warheads permitted on each MIRVed missile.

With respect to new land-based missiles, each side has agreed to limit its deployment of new ICBMs to one type over the term of the treaty. The agreement's definition of a "new type" of missile, however, will not necessarily require that either side stop developing all but one new generation of land-based missile, since new missiles do not have to count as a "new type" if they are substantially the same as the older generation they replace. For example, the Soviets' new "fifth generation" systems, which have not yet been fully tested, may in the end not be limited at all by this provision. But if the Soviets act as expected and use their allowance of one new ICBM type to develop a single warhead missile to replace their existing SS-11s, any "modernization" of their land-base MIRV force with a new "fifth generation" will result in replacing existing missiles with new missiles of very similar dimensions and propulsion characteristics.

The number of reentry vehicles (warheads) on each new type of MIRVed missile will be limited by the new agreement to something no greater than ten on ICBMs (the exact limits are not yet agreed) and to 14 on SLBMs. The number of warheads on each existing type of missile is frozen at its present level. These provisions solve a major military problem for U.S. force planners, making a "multiple aim point" (MAP) system—having more hardened shelters than there are missiles with the missiles clandestinely shuffled about among the shelters—at least theoretically feasible for the United States. Without such a limit, proliferating the number of aim points (targets) that the Soviet Union would have to attack if it wished to destroy our land-based missile force could lead to no more than a continuing race between our deployment of additional aim points and the Soviets' deployment of additional warheads. But the treaty will restrain the number of Soviet counterforce warheads to a practical limit of about 9,000, setting this as the worst case situation for which U.S. force planners might have to prepare.

As these examples illustrate, on the whole the United States has achieved almost every negotiating objective it set during the last year. This is also true with respect to its objectives in the important area of verification constraints.

The Verification Issue

The Soviets have maintained from the beginning of the SALT process that the only provisions necessary to ensure adequate verification were those contained in the SALT I agreement: prohibitions on deliberate concealment and on interference with "national technical means" of verification. The United States, on the other hand, has argued that a variety of "counting rules" and "collateral constraints" are necessary to permit U.S. verification of Soviet compliance. The Soviets have strongly opposed such an approach, primarily because the U.S. proposals would require significant modifications in Soviet deployment programs, while requiring no changes at all in U.S. programs.

Nevertheless, the Soviets have now agreed to two important "counting rules" related to MIRVed missiles, accepted in principle the important concept of "functionally related observable differences (FRODs)," agreed to terminate their SS-16 mobile ICBM program for verification reasons, and accepted an important principle on the concealment of testing results relevant to verification. Furthermore, by dropping their demand for a 2,500 kilometer upper limit on the range of air-launched cruise missiles, they have eased the problem of verifying cruise-missile range limits.

The agreement concerning the SS-16 land-based mobile ICBM provides a useful illustration of the extent to which the Soviets have been willing to accept provisions designed to facilitate verification, as well as the thoroughness with which the provisions of the treaty have been worked out. The issue arises because of the similarity of the SS-16 to the SS-20, a mobile intermediate-range ballistic missile (IRBM) capable of hitting targets in China and Europe, but not the United States. The SS-20 is apparently only a shortened version of the SS-16—the two missile stages of the SS-20 are identical to the first two stages of the three-stage SS-16. Furthermore, the mobile launchers for the two systems are almost identical.

This situation led the United States to worry that an SS-16 ICBM deployment could not be distinguished from an SS-20 IRBM deployment by satellite verification methods. The SS-16 missile is considerably less capable than the other new Soviet missiles (SS-17s, SS-18s, and SS-19s); nonetheless, such a clandestine deployment would give the Soviets a certain advantage. In any event, the uncertainty about the size of the Soviet program would lead to continuing arguments about Soviet compliance with the treaty.

It has been reported that the Soviets have agreed to ban the deployment of the SS-16 as a mobile missile for the duration of the treaty, a provision that apparently eliminates the problem of distinguishing between the two systems. But if this were the extent of the treaty's handling of this problem, the provision would still be susceptible to criticism. The Soviets could continue testing and producing the SS-16 missile without deploying it in a mobile mode, and the launchers for the missile could be produced and deployed under the guise of the SS-20. Such a state of affairs would leave the Soviets only a few weeks away from being able to deploy an operational SS-16 ICBM system.

The final agreement, however, provides stronger assurance that the United States can verify compliance with this aspect of the treaty. The Soviets have now agreed to ban *all* deployment of the SS-16, whether in a mobile mode or at fixed sites. They have further agreed to ban the production of all missile components that are unique to the SS-16 ICBM version and to cease testing the SS-16. These provisions eliminate the possibility of developing a capability to deploy rapidly the SS-16 should the treaty be abrogated.

While the new agreement is by and large extremely comprehensive in its verification provisions, one notable absence is a rigorous definition of a missile launcher. In order to eliminate any possible ambiguity about the meaning of other provisions, such a definition should be agreed upon by the two sides. However, the United States has resisted the inclusion of such a definition, apparently because it would be difficult to write one that drew any distinction between the unMIRVed Minuteman II missile silos and the

MIRVed Minuteman III silos, and because such a definition might stand in the way of an American multiple aim point ICBM-basing system.

The Minuteman II and Minuteman III silos are so similar that almost any conceivable definition would result in their both being classified as a single-launcher type. Since we have pressed for and gotten Soviet agreement to a "counting rule" requiring that any launcher of a type that has ever launched a MIRVed missile be counted as containing a MIRVed missile, a launcher definition that did not distinguish between Minuteman II and Minuteman III silos would require that we count all 450 single-warhead Minuteman II missiles within the treaty's ceilings on MIRV launchers—an unacceptable result.

The lack of a precise definition of a launcher is also important to protect America's option to deploy a multiple aim point system. As described earlier, such a system relies on the deployment of a greater number of hardened shelters than missiles, with the missiles being moved clandestinely from one shelter to another. If the "shelters" were actually additional missile silos, an approach now favored by the Air Force, and if the silos themselves were counted as "launchers," they would be prohibited under provisions carried over from SALT I banning new land-based ICBM launchers. But in the U.S. interpretation, the new agreement does not ban a multiple aim point system, because the transportable capsule containing the missile is considered the launcher, rather than the silo itself.

This is one of several examples in the new agreement where the United States has sacrificed its principles in order to avoid a constraint on its programs. In this particular case, the Soviets do not appear concerned about their ability to verify U.S. MIRV deployments; thus, they have been willing to "look the other way." One can only hope that in the end the Soviets do not attempt to take advantage of the agreement's ambiguous definition of a launcher, leading us to wish we had insisted upon a more explicit resolution of the problem.

Obtaining Soviet agreement on these verification provisions involved considerably more than convincing them to accept a set of abstract principles. The verification provisions of the new treaty will actually constrain Soviet programs. The SS-16 mobile ICBM, which was fully tested and ready for deployment, will have to be abandoned altogether. The fully tested single-warhead versions of the SS-17 and SS-18 missiles, some of which may have already been deployed, will either have to be counted as MIRVed missiles or abandoned. Finally, the Soviets probably have 120 unMIRVed missiles now deployed in modernized silos that will have to count as MIRVed missiles unless they are moved to other silos, since the silos they are now in are the same as those used to launch the MIRVed SS-19.

On balance, the new agreement embodies a sensible approach to verification. It implicitly acknowledges that any verification requires cooperation of the two sides, not only in general measures such as noninterference and non-concealment, but in specific instances as well. By including specific verification provisions, our job is made easier; in many cases, we must verify only that the cooperative procedures are being complied with, rather than verifying compliance with the treaty directly. Finally, the treaty embodies an important shift in the emphasis of the SALT process, with relatively more weight being given to what it is we wish to limit as opposed to what limits we could most easily verify. Only a few years ago, there was almost unanimous agreement among experts that once MIRVs had been fully tested, limits on MIRVed missiles could not be verified. But such limits are one of the most important results of the SALT II agreement. It is gratifying that we sought and achieved limits on MIRVs, albeit modest ones, despite the difficulties in verification which required working out explicit "counting rules."

Impact on Strategic Balance

As discussed earlier, one cannot adequately evaluate the new treaty without considering its effect on the strategic balance between the United States and the U.S.S.R. The simplest measures of the strategic balance are "static" indicators of force quantities, such as numbers of launchers, numbers of weapons, megatonnage, "equivalent" megatonnage, throw-weight, and so forth. Projections are that the Soviets will lead the United States by 1980 in most of these static indicators, although the United States will retain a significant lead in the total number of weapons deployed.

The weaknesses inherent in attempting to measure the strategic balance using static indicators are well known. These indicators do not account for some of the most important characteristics of our forces, such as their survivability against a Soviet attack. It is for exactly this reason that U.S. force planners have consistently chosen not to attempt to match the Soviets in such measures, but rather to emphasize more important force characteristics. Nevertheless, it is worth pointing out that under the terms of the agreement, the United States could essentially match the Soviet Union in each of the commonly used static indicators of force capability, should it choose to do so. The one unequal limit in the new agreement is the freeze on "heavy" land-based missiles carried over from SALT I. Under this provision, the United States is prohibited from deploying heavy missiles, while the Soviet Union may keep the 300 it now has. Thus, the Soviets could, in theory, deploy four to five million pounds more land-based missile throw-weight than could this country, although the United States could offset this somewhat with additional throw-weight in its submarine-launched ballistic missiles or payload in its bombers. But, in practice, the United States has no interest in heavy missiles, so this apparent asymmetry is of little importance.

A more sophisticated approach to assessing the strategic balance is to examine the results of simulated force exchanges between the two countries. The United States has accepted for many years the notion that the most important criterion for assessing the adequacy of its strategic forces is that enough forces be able to withstand a Soviet surprise attack to destroy Soviet society and industry in retaliation. There is little argument about either the present or projected capability of U.S. forces to carry out this mission, with or without SALT II. But there are serious arguments about whether such an "assured destruction" scenario is the proper one for measuring the deterrent capacity of our forces, and whether our forces will remain adequate when their capability is assessed under more complex scenarios.

Until the Soviets began deploying MIRVs on their land-based missiles in 1973, the United States maintained an overwhelming superiority in its strategic forces. Furthermore, the SALT I treaty prohibiting antiballistic missile systems (ABMs) meant that U.S. ballistic missiles could attack the Soviet Union in a retaliatory strike without facing the uncertainties associated with having to penetrate enemy defenses. Under such circumstances, there was little reason to use complex force exchange scenarios in assessing the deterrent capacity of the U.S. force.

The advent of large, accurate MIRVs on Soviet missiles changed this situation. The extensive Soviet MIRV deployment program, coming on the heels of SALT I and the beginning of what was supposed to be a period of détente, and occurring simultaneously with Soviet initiatives in Vietnam, the Middle East, and Africa, has led to a widespread questioning of Soviet motives. I have argued elsewhere that the Soviets had good military reasons for deploying large throw-weight land-based MIRVed missiles; one does not have to attribute to them a motive of attempting to achieve strategic superiority over the United States to explain these deployments. But the new Soviet MIRVs do create real military problems for the United States: for the first time, the Soviets appear headed for a capability to attack a major component of the U.S. deterrent force—our land-based ICBMs.

It is important to emphasize that most military planners are concerned only secondarily with what might happen once a nuclear war began. The level of destruction of any nuclear war would be so overwhelming that the primary focus must of necessity be on our ability to deter the start of any war. Thus, the concern is not so much that the Soviets might actually attempt a surprise attack against our Minuteman force, although military planners obviously must consider such an eventuality. Rather, the issue is the ability of our strategic nuclear forces to serve as a "nuclear umbrella" in a crisis, given the Soviets' newfound capability to attack our land-based ICBMs.

First Strike Capabilities

In the mid-1980s, the Soviets will be able theoretically to destroy virtually all of our land-based ICBM force in a surprise attack. This would leave us with only our submarine-launched ballistic missile force, our strategic bomber force (equipped with air-launched cruise missiles), and our theater nuclear forces deployed overseas and on aircraft carriers. Some of these forces are also susceptible to attack, since not all U.S. bombers are on alert at any one time, some submarines are in port, and many of our theater nuclear forces are vulnerable. Nevertheless, even in the worst case, 5,000 to 6,000 nuclear weapons on alert bombers and submarines at sea would survive a surprise attack.

This force is more than enough to destroy all major Soviet cities and Soviet industry. But defense planners argue, with good reason, that in such a situation, no President of the United States would want to be faced with only the options of doing nothing or launching an all-out attack on Soviet cities—an attack that would almost certainly lead to a Soviet counterstrike against U.S. cities, presumably left largely undamaged by the Soviets' earlier strike against our land-based ICBMs. Many argue that in such circumstances, the United States would be deterred from retaliating by the Soviets' retention of a large residual "assured destruction" force after attacking our Minuteman force.

I find two weaknesses in this line of thought. First, in the mid-1980s the United States will have the capability to respond to a Soviet counterforce attack with a counterforce response of its own. The United States will have 2,000 to 3,000 highly accurate cruise missiles deployed on its alert bombers, each having 50–80 percent probability of destroying any hardened target against which it is launched. These weapons could be used in a counterforce retaliation while still leaving the alert U.S. SLBM force, with 3,000 weapons, as an "assured destruction" reserve.

Cruise missiles do have two deficiencies when used in a counterforce attack. First, they require many hours to reach their targets, making them less flexible than ICBMs, which have more "prompt" effects. Second, the Soviets could easily destroy most U.S. airfields in an initial strike, which would require a U.S. President to use his cruise missiles immediately afted a full-scale Soviet attack while they remain airborne, or risk their loss. But these deficiencies are relatively minor. If the Soviets' initial attack against our Minutemen were less than all-out, surviving land-based missiles would be available for selective counterforce attacks. We would find ourselves without surviving land-based missiles, and thus without the capability to launch "prompt" counterforce attacks, only after a very large Soviet attack—a circumstance under which no U.S. President should have any hesitance about launching an all-out cruise missile counterforce retaliatory attack.

The second fallacy in using a Soviet first-strike "war-fighting" scenario to evaluate the U.S. deterrent stems from a failure to consider the situation a Soviet leader would face should he consider using his counterforce threat to extract U.S. concessions. While there are uncertainties both in force exchange calculation and in force projections for 1985, the Soviets will in all likelihood face a significantly greater potential loss from a U.S. preemptive strike than the United States would face from a Soviet preemptive strike. This stems directly from the Soviets' decision to place the majority of their forces in land-based silos, which will be vulnerable to attack in the mid-1980s. The United States has long recognized this problem and has put relatively less emphasis on its land-based missile force. By this time, the U.S. land-based missile force will be able to destroy 80 to 90 percent of the Soviet land-based MIRVed missile force in a preemptive strike, even if no new land-based missile is deployed. If the new MX missile (a land-based missile that would carry six to ten weapons, each of one to two megatons yield) is deployed, the United States could destroy virtually all Soviet land-based missiles, MIRVed and single warhead, in such a strike. Soviet submarines in port and Soviet bomber bases could also be destroyed. Thus, the Soviets could well face a situation where they had lost the mainstay of their force, their MIRVed land-based missiles, while the United States retained 7,000–9,000 weapons on its submarines and bombers. If one believes that the prospect of retaining an inadequate residual reserve force after absorbing a first strike would deter American Presidents from acting firmly in confrontations with the Soviet Union, a Soviet leader should be even more deterred from initiating a confrontation since he would face an even less favorable situation.

Although the Soviet deployment of a counterforce capability against our Minuteman missiles does not leave the United States at a relative disadvantage, it does give a more significant military advantage to the side striking first than has been the case previously, reducing the inherent stability of the nuclear balance. A preemptive strike by either side would risk an immediate retaliation that could destroy most of the attacker's society, so war is still an unlikely event. Nevertheless, in an extreme crisis, such

as that which might grow out of a gradual escalation of
hostilities in Europe or the Middle East, the world would
be safer if neither side felt it could achieve any significant
advantage by launching a preemptive strike.

The preferable solution to this problem would be to
obtain Soviet agreement in SALT III to reduce fixed-point
land-based missile deployments. To date, the Soviets have
rejected U.S. proposals for such reductions, although past
U.S. proposals have tended to be somewhat one-sided in
their relatively greater effect on Soviet programs. The
Soviets have already accepted separate limits on land-
based MIRVed missiles in SALT II, and they have agreed
to principles for SALT III calling for reductions and increasing mutual confidence in the stability of the nuclear
balance. Thus, it is not inconceivable that they would
negotiate a balanced proposal for ICBM reductions.

But unless the Soviets agree early in SALT III to significant reductions in land-based ICBMs, the strategic balance in the mid-1980s is likely to be determined to a much
greater extent by the force deployment programs of the
two sides than it is by the provisions of arms control agreements. Thus, it is important that the United States retain
the flexibility it needs to undertake programs that will
maintain this balance. Perhaps the most extensive program
suggested to date has been that outlined by the Committee
on the Present Danger, a citizens' group organized to support a stronger U.S. response to the Soviet military buildup.
Stating their position that "in the short run, it is unlikely
that a comprehensive SALT agreement can be negotiated,"
the Committee has recommended an eight-point program
for restoring "both real and perceived strategic adequacy
for the 1980s":

1. Urgent attention to the survivability and endurance of our
   information, communications, and command and control systems;
2. Rapid deployment of an alternate basing mode for our
   ICBMs;

3. Development of a more capable follow-on missile to replace our Minuteman IIIs;
4. Procurement of a high quality strategic bomber and cruise missile-tanker system with high pre-launch survivability and penetrability;
5. Acceleration of the TRIDENT I SLBM deployment program, TRIDENT II development, and, if possible, TRIDENT submarine construction, and renewed study and development of a smaller SLBM submarine;
6. Rehabilitation of the air defense program with AWACS, F-14/Phoenix, and new surface-to-air missiles;
7. Reexamination of the token U.S. civil defense program;
8. Reinvigoration of ABM research and development programs.

Non-Limits of SALT II

One may or may not agree with the wisdom of the particular measures suggested by the Committee. But in assessing the effect of SALT II on the strategic balance, it is important to note that the new agreement does not prohibit the United States from carrying out any of these recommendations; all eight could be fully implemented under the terms of the agreement. As much as one might believe that the United States needs a larger strategic nuclear defense program, one cannot argue that SALT II will stand in the way of even extensive force enhancement programs such as this one.

SALT II has already stimulated considerable debate within the NATO alliance. The U.S. allies clearly see a stronger relationship between their security interests and the terms of the emerging agreement than was the case with SALT I. During SALT I, the allies' primary concern was to ensure that existing nuclear cooperation and technology transfer programs would not be jeopardized. The inclusion in SALT II of only very general "noncircumvention" provisions seems to ensure that the new agreement will pose no problems in this regard, especially since the United States explicitly rejected the more restrictive language constraining transfers of weapons technology proposed by the Soviets.

But since SALT I, the Soviets have deployed longer range tactical aircraft capable of launching nuclear attacks in Europe, the new SS-20 mobile intermediate-range ballistic missile with MIRVs, and the Backfire aircraft—an aircraft somewhat more capable than the F-111, our largest aircraft in Europe. At the same time that these deployments have occurred, the Soviets have moved to overall parity with the United States in intercontinental nuclear forces, reducing the Europeans' confidence in the capability of the U.S. "strategic nuclear umbrella" to deter Soviet attacks on them. These two events have stimulated considerable anxiety in Europe, particularly in the Federal Republic of Germany.

The difficulties associated with attempting to accommodate in arms control negotiations the "gray area" systems, such as U.S. forward-based systems and Soviet intermediate-range ballistic missiles and medium bombers, have been analyzed extensively elsewhere. My objective here is not to repeat this analysis, but rather simply to suggest that the problem of providing an adequate nuclear defense for Europe goes well beyond any difficulties the Europeans might have with the specific limits included in SALT II. This is not to claim that SALT II has no effect on Europe. The treaty does not include limits on systems such as the Backfire and the SS-20 IRBM, while it does limit U.S. SLBMs, some of which are specifically dedicated to the defense of Europe and intended to offset these Soviet systems. The three-year protocol to the treaty also limits cruise missiles, which might be used to enhance NATO's "Euro-strategic" nuclear balance. The Europeans correctly perceive a Soviet effort through SALT to limit weapons systems seen as Europe's main hope for offsetting any advantage the Soviets might obtain through their recent SS-20 and Backfire deployments, without the Soviets accepting any limits on their own deployments; the United States must be sensitive to this legitimate European concern.

To a large extent, the United States has brought about the Europeans' present state of anxiety with respect to SALT II. The United States has certainly not spoken with a single voice in its consultation with the Europeans on SALT II and theater nuclear programs. U.S. officials responsible for the SALT negotiations have tended to downplay the significance of land-based and sea-based long-range cruise missiles, while at the same time Pentagon officials have extolled the virtues of cruise missiles to their European counterparts. The fact is that ground-launched and sea-launched cruise missiles have significant weaknesses as nuclear weapons for use in the European theater. While the cruise missiles themselves are relatively inexpensive, the total systems, including the sea-based platforms to carry them and the ground-based launchers and associated systems, are not likely to be significantly less expensive than alternative nuclear systems. Furthermore, no reliable concepts have been developed for solving the pre-launch vulnerability problem of ground-launched cruise missiles. Hardened fixed sites will be vulnerable to Soviet attack, but serious problems exist in attempting to deploy long-range mobile nuclear systems in densely populated Western Europe. Moving nuclear-armed missiles throughout the West German countryside in peacetime is unthinkable, yet stationing them in *kasernes* renders them vulnerable to surprise attack. Deployments on surface ships face similar vulnerability problems, and deployments on submarines would divert valuable antisubmarine warfare systems to a less useful military mission.

All apart from the relative worth of cruise missiles as "Euro-strategic" nuclear weapons, the basic strategic dilemma associated with providing an independent European force to counter the Soviet theater-oriented forces remains much the same as it has been for the last 20 years. As long as the U.S. President controls the release of the bulk of NATO's strategic nuclear weapons, their use would immediately involve the United States in a strategic exchange with the Soviet Union, with all of the implications, both positive and negative, which that linkage involves. As the French have long realized, for a European deterrent to be truly independent, the Europeans must have complete control of it. Yet no one suspects that West Germany either desires to have or should have its own independent nuclear force, and many Europeans doubt the inherent wisdom of "decoupling" from the U.S. strategic deterrent in any event.

Overcoming European Anxieties

In my view, a threefold set of actions on the part of the United States is necessary to overcome our allies' anxiety created by the growing Soviet Euro-strategic capabilities, the fading of the boundary in SALT between intercontinental and theater forces, and continuing concern over "decoupling." First, the United States must play a more assertive and consistent leadership role in alliance nuclear affairs and demonstrate increased sensitivity to legitimate European defense needs. The enhanced radiation warhead (neutron bomb) affair provides an excellent example of how these almost trite principles seem to have been overlooked in recent months. The United States put the issue to the German government for decision in such a way that it was inevitably propelled into a public debate. The German government was required to choose between rejecting a weapon it thought might be important to Germany's defense (although they would have to look to the United States for a more thorough technical judgment in this respect), or accepting the domestic political consequences of pushing for a new weapon that had come to have particularly distasteful moral implications in the public mind. The German political system, especially while the Social Democratic Party is in power, simply could not be expected to generate a rational policy under such circumstances.

Second, our European allies must more thoroughly accept, nearly 20 years after it was first put forth, the proposition that the "nuclear umbrella" can only go so far in providing adequate security for Europe. The best way to enhance European security is to improve Europe's own conventional defense capability, and any available additional European defense resources should be allocated principally to this task.

Finally, the United States must make clear to the Soviets that large-scale SS-20 and Backfire deployments will be met by comparable U.S. programs—either cruise missiles, extended-range Pershing deployments, or additional nuclear-capable aircraft—unless the Soviets agree to reasonable limits on their "Euro-strategic" forces, or demonstrate unilateral restraint. While one might allow that too many exclusively European-based American nuclear forces could lead to an undesirable "decoupling" of the U.S. strategic deterrent, it seems clear that too extreme an imbalance in the other direction would also have a similar "decoupling" effect. An overwhelming local nuclear superiority might well tempt the Soviets in a confrontation to assume that their intercontinental forces could deter U.S. intercontinental forces, leading them to push for concessions in Europe. Thus, it is absolutely unrealistic for the Soviets to expect the United States to accept SALT III limits on systems useful primarily in the European theater without restraints being placed on comparable Soviet systems.

If the United States adopts a firm position on these issues in SALT III, there should be little need for complicated new forums for negotiating "gray area" systems. As I discuss in the concluding section, the Soviets are likely to agree to negotiate on Euro-strategic forces in SALT III as the three-year protocol limiting deployment of long-range ground-based and sea-based cruise missiles nears expiration. If U.S. programs make it clear to the Soviets that this country fully intends to deploy new systems designed to redress the imbalance in Euro-strategic forces created by Backfire and SS-20 deployments, the Soviets should be willing to negotiate reasonable limits on these systems.

Important Precedents

The new SALT agreement is, in many respects, more than the sum of its individual provisions. It differs significantly from its predecessors in both its form and in its basic approach, and it sets important precedents for the future.

It is important to review the history of SALT in order to compare the two approaches. SALT I consisted of two parts: a permanent treaty banning antiballistic missile systems (ABMs), and a five-year interim agreement freezing deployment levels of strategic missiles. The ABM treaty has caused very little controversy and remains the preeminent achievement of SALT to date. Without ABMs, it is virtually impossible for either side to eliminate the retaliatory deterrent force of the other side. We have the luxury to debate issues such as the importance of emerging Minuteman vulnerability only because the ABM treaty exists. If both sides had proceeded with antiballistic missile programs, the stability of our deterrent would be dramatically reduced, and the size of the deployment program needed to maintain our deterrent correspondingly increased.

The criticisms of SALT I focused on the offensive forces agreement. Even during the negotiating process, there was considerable controversy concerning whether or not any attempt at all should be made to negotiate offensive limits. In the end, it was the United States that insisted upon the linkage between the offensive agreement and the ABM treaty. The Nixon Administration argued that achieving any offensive forces agreement was a major accomplishment since the Soviets were deploying new missiles at a rapid rate, while the United States had no new deployments underway. Thus, it was argued that the interim offensive agreement stopped the Soviet deployment program, while having no effect on U.S. programs.

Nevertheless, the critics, led by Senator Henry Jackson, focused on the offensive agreement, particularly on the fact that the ban on additional launchers left missile launchers frozen at unequal levels for the two sides—approximately 2,400 for the Soviet Union, versus 1,700 for the United States. Later, further controversy arose on two grounds. First, the terms of the agreement itself proved subject to differing interpretations. Terms such as "light missile" and "deliberate concealment" were interpreted quite differently by the United States and the Soviet Union. Second, it quickly became apparent that limiting deployments of new missile launchers had very little effect on the offensive arms race between the two countries. Both sides continued modernizing their forces, with the Soviets pursuing an aggressive program of replacing older single-warhead missiles with larger more capable MIRVed ICBMs.

Since SALT I, there has been considerable debate concerning the best way to proceed with offensive force limitations. Some have argued that the focus on quantitative limits is not itself a problem, but that the limits imposed so far are simply too high to have any effect. Others have argued that massive reductions are not in the cards and perhaps not even desirable, and that only a direct assault on advancing technology through limits on qualitative force characteristics can be of any real arms control use. Finally, some have argued that the greatest utility of SALT is likely to come from ruling out destabilizing missions, such as hard target counterforce, or, at a minimum, focusing on measures that will enhance strategic stability, such as limiting the numbers of land-based MIRVs—the weapons that could most easily be used to attack the land-based ICBMs of the other side.

The new treaty at least takes steps toward meeting almost all of these earlier objections. The numerical limits are equal for both sides, which meets Senator Jackson's main criticism of SALT I. The final numerical limits have been reduced from those agreed at Vladivostok and represent a real constraint on future Soviet programs, even requiring that the Soviets dismantle over 250 older systems. Even though the numerical limits themselves still leave room for increases in the capabilities of each side through qualitative improvements, they do eliminate the "worst case" projections of future force levels which would otherwise be considered by force planners in each country. Finally, the new agreement does represent an evolution of SALT in the direction the United States has long argued that SALT must go if it is to continue to play a significant role in stabilizing the nuclear balance. There are modest but significant qualitative limits in the treaty, through the ban on more than one new type of ICBM and the ceilings on the number of weapons each missile or bomber can carry. Furthermore, the various limits on land-based ICBMs, as well as the continuation of the ABM treaty, demonstrate at least an implicit acceptance of the basic U.S. strategic view that insuring the survival of secure second-strike retaliatory forces even after a first strike should be SALT's major military contribution.

The new SALT treaty also demonstrates an implicit understanding and acknowledgment of the limits of arms control agreements. Strategic arms agreements will not eliminate nuclear weapons, or even eliminate the military problems faced by the United States in maintaining its deterrent capability against the Soviet Union. The best we can hope for is that they will moderate the competition, reduce the level of hostility, and clarify the intentions of each side. In the long run, it can be hoped that such agreements will set firm limits on the total nuclear capabilities of each side, effectively stopping the arms race. But they cannot, as was attempted by the Administration's March 1977 "comprehensive" proposal, redress what we perceive to be Soviet advantages in the strategic balance—at least not without our offering major concessions in terms of our deployment programs.

Perhaps the solution to this problem is inherent in another new direction set by this treaty when compared to SALT I. By including a set of principles for governing SALT III, the new agreement establishes SALT as an ongoing process, rather than as an individual treaty required to stand by itself. Since many of the limitations accepted by the Soviet Union in the negotiation of SALT II represent at least implicit acceptance of arms control principles the United States has always put forward (adequate verification, emphasis on protecting the deterrent forces of the two sides, rigorous definitions, mutual exchange of data, and true limits on overall force capabilities), there remains substantial hope that SALT III will be able to constrain new programs before they are so far underway that the vested interests and bureaucracies on each side make it impossible to curb them.

Refuting the Critics

Much of the criticism of SALT II has focused either on the specific provisions of the Vladivostok accord on which the agreement is based, or on the deficiencies of the treaty when compared to the more ambitious "comprehensive" approach set forth by the Administration in March 1977. But if one puts aside preconceptions based on these earlier efforts and examines the treaty which has actually been negotiated, it is difficult to see how it can be opposed on its technical merits. The treaty embodies a substantial amount of "true arms control," in that it requires actual dismantling of some Soviet systems, cuts off certain areas of possible new competition, and eliminates the "worst case" force projections which have tended to drive the deployment programs of each side. At the same time, the new agreement does not stand in the way of necessary defense programs. It permits the United States to carry on with any necessary modernization of its strategic triad, whether it be a new bomber or cruise missile carrier, a multiple-aim-point system of ICBM launchers, a new land-based missile, or new types of submarine-launched ballistic missiles. The treaty language is extremely carefully drafted, so that subsequent misunderstandings between the two sides should be small in number, especially when compared to those which occurred in SALT I, and the Soviets have accepted the special verification "counting rules" sought by the United States. The treaty should provide a framework within which the United States can develop a stable strategic program to respond to recent Soviet deployments, knowing that major surprises in the Soviet program are unlikely to occur. This should permit setting aside the present diversionary debate over strategic forces and moving on to focus our defense planning on correcting more serious weaknesses in conventional forces.

Given these technical characteristics of the new agreement, the debate over treaty ratification is likely to focus on predominantly political questions. There is a legitimate issue about whether or not the United States should enter into any additional agreements with the Soviet Union as long as the Soviets continue with their worldwide military buildup and expansionist policies. There will also be a political debate about the relationship between the new agreement and the defense budget, with some arguing that the treaty is unacceptable without a significant increase in the defense budget, including approval of major new strategic nuclear programs, and others cautioning against linking treaty approval to increased defense spending, lest we mortgage our ability to proceed with further arms control measures. Finally, there will be considerable debate about the treaty's three-year protocol.

The protocol will cause particular concern because it limits weapons systems which could potentially be of vital importance to the United States in overcoming what are perhaps the two most significant strategic nuclear problems the nation will face in the 1980s. The protocol limits the testing and deployment of mobile land-based ICBMs (such as the multiple-aim-point system discussed earlier), systems whose main purpose would be to eliminate the emerging vulnerability of our Minuteman ICBMs. The protocol also limits ground-launched and sea-launched cruise missiles, systems proposed primarily to counter the growing imbalance in Euro-strategic forces brought about by Soviet deployments of new systems such as the Backfire and the SS-20. Given the potential importance that mobile ICBMs and cruise missiles could have for the U.S. defense program, any agreement placing limits on these systems would be controversial. The fact that the protocol contains no reciprocal limits on Soviet systems, such as the SS-20 or the Backfire, makes it even more controversial.

As I have pointed out earlier, the protocol will expire before the United States could conceivably deploy any of the systems limited by it, so that in a technical sense, it represents no real constraint on U.S. programs. But it is always difficult politically for the United States to end a deployment moratorium, since the American public never wishes to support what might be seen as unnecessary military competition. Moreover, the protocol does set a precedent for U.S. acceptance of continuing limits on cruise missiles and mobile land-based ICBMs in SALT III.

My own view is that in the absence of a serious SALT III negotiation, political pressures will not inevitably require the United States to continue with the protocol limits. But the Soviets are unlikely to turn down a serious SALT III negotiation, or even to reject a negotiation that includes the important questions of the Euro-strategic balance and Minuteman vulnerability. Initially, they will resist U.S. demands in these areas. But as the expiration of the protocol nears, they will offer enough tangible concessions to induce the United States to extend the protocol's moratoria as the negotiations continue. For the United States, there would be great benefit in obtaining a negotiated solution to the problems of Minuteman vulnerability and Euro-strategic balance, since the deployment of cruise missiles in Europe or a mobile ICBM in the United States are not attractive options from a technical standpoint. Thus, if the protocol serves to engage the Soviets in a serious negotiation on these issues, it will have served a useful purpose. One can only hope that the United States will remain firm in its insistence that the Soviets agree to serious and balanced provisions in both areas, rather than continuing the protocol limits indefinitely while the Soviets continue to threaten both our land-based ICBMs and our European allies.

Renewed U.S. Will

Most of the political issues raised by SALT II, including the protocol limitations, relate to a more fundamental concern that the United States has lost its will to maintain adequate defenses in the face of Soviet expansion. The strong anti-defense reaction brought about by the years of Vietnam and Watergate, and the hopes that détente with the Soviet Union would mean a greater degree of Soviet restraint in weapons deployments and geopolitical expansionism, led to a period of perhaps excessive reductions in real defense spending. But recent events indicate that this trend has now ended, and that there is a strong and increasing national will to maintain adequate defenses. Public opinion polls indicate that the American people are willing to support higher spending on defense, despite the growing negative reaction to government spending in general and the emergence of the "taxpayer's revolt." President Carter has successfully increased the defense budget and is publicly committed to a three percent annual real growth in our spending on defense. Nor is there any evidence that

Congress will oppose necessary defense spending; the defense appropriations veto fight that occurred this year was not over the level of spending, but rather over the best way to spend the available dollars.

Even if one believes that the nation's main defense problem is the need to demonstrate a strong will to respond to Soviet force deployments and geopolitical expansion, it is not at all clear that Senate rejection of the SALT II agreement would demonstrate such will. If the treaty contained serious technical flaws, or if it explicitly prohibited necessary defense programs, its rejection would perhaps be seen as a demonstration of renewed American strength. But this agreement does not contain such deficiencies. Therefore, in my view its rejection would more likely convey a different set of signals. It would indicate first of all that the U.S. political system cannot generate a stable national consensus on even the most crucial foreign policy issues. Second, rejection would make it clear to our allies that a relaxation of East-West tensions is not likely to come about from bilateral U.S.-U.S.S.R. negotiations; thus, if they wish to pursue a political détente, they will have to do so on their own. Finally, a rejection would imply that we have no confidence in our own defense programs—that we are seriously worried about our military position relative to that of the Soviet Union, and feel that even the modest limits within the treaty would stand in the way of redressing any imbalance.

If there were no other reason to accept the new treaty than to avoid the negative consequences which might flow from its rejection, one could hardly expect more than reluctant acquiescence of either the Senate or the American public. But the new treaty deserves more than this. As this essay has argued, it is a treaty very much in the U.S. interest, and it sets important and positive precedents for a continuation of the SALT process. Given the quality of the treaty, its rejection would lead the rest of the world to see the United States as hesitant, insecure, and incapable of mounting an effective political and military effort to establish a stable peace in the nuclear age.

WHY SALT II DESERVES SUPPORT[4]

We begin a deadly serious subject with a fantasy:

WHEELING, W.Va. (AP)—Senator Jack D. Ripper, the retired NATO commander, today announced his candidacy for president in 1984, accusing the administration of 'blindness bordering on treason' for 'letting Russia gain decisive nuclear superiority' over the US. He said the administration had 'ignored secret studies showing the Soviets are hiding thousands and thousands of new-type super-missiles with up to 40 warheads each.' Administration sources discounted reports of such Soviet activity, but Ripper claimed the studies show big, new missiles are being hidden 'in caves, under tarpaulins, in wells, wherever the Soviets can conceal them.' He declared, 'America faces a survival gap' and called for drastic cuts in social spending to support a $350-billion 'crash' defense and civil defense program. 'Every American should pledge to "Beat Russia, Save America," ' Ripper declared to the cheers and chants of thousands. 'Those who won't can only be suspected of wanting Russia to beat us. . . .'

It is a fantasy that the dizzy Air Force colonel in *Dr. Strangelove* could rise to be a general, NATO commander, senator and presidential contender and would announce his candidacy in the same city where Joseph McCarthy began witch-hunting for subversives in 1950. But it is not fantasy—rather, it is history—that when the United States does not know what the Soviet Union is doing in nuclear weaponry, it begins fearing the worst, and then believes it. "Secret studies" in the 1950s and early 1960s gave us "bomber gaps" and "missile gaps" that didn't exist. Officials who discounted the studies were branded as blind and weak.

[4] From article entitled "We Support SALT." *New Republic*. 180:5–10. My. 5, '79. Reprinted by permission of THE NEW REPUBLIC, © 1979 The New Republic, Inc.

Expensive defense and civil defense programs were insti-
tuted on a crisis basis. And in the cold war environment,
fear of the Soviet Union did lead to loyalty tests, pledges
and other civil liberties depredations.

Could it happen again? Perhaps not exactly as before,
but we suspect that Senate defeat of the forthcoming SALT
2 treaty with the Soviet Union *would* lead to worst-case
assumptions about Soviet capabilities and intentions, expensive compensatory US programs, and a poisonous political environment both internationally and at home. To
avoid these consequences—and, above all, to avoid stumbling into cold war and nuclear war—we favor ratification
of the treaty. The full text of the treaty is not yet available
(though most details are) and we do not rule out the
possibility that the ratification debate could turn up de-
cisively damaging new informaton. But on the basis of what
we know, we think the treaty—though far from providing
the US absolute security—is much better than no treaty at
all.

SALT's Main Virtue

The main virtue of SALT is that it provides a base line
for judging what the Soviets are up to. It establishes rules
for what they can build and what they can't. If the treaty is
ratified, the Soviets (and we) will be bound to limit our
total number of strategic launch vehicles (missiles and
bombers) to 2400 at first, and then to 2250 by the end of
1981. The treaty contains separate limits for missiles
equipped with multiple warheads and specific, detailed prohibitions against building new heavy missiles, increasing
the number of warheads each missile can carry, and developing more than one new kind of missile between now
and 1985. Moreover, the treaty forbids interference with our
ability to verify Soviet missile developments by satellite
and electronic ground stations. So we will know how many
strategic weapons the Soviet Union is supposed to have, and
of what type. If we find they have anything that is more

and different, we can accuse them of cheating and (if it comes to that) threaten to renounce, or actually renounce, the treaty. But without a treaty, there will be no standards, no limits, no rules against concealment. We would have to assume the worst about what they were doing, and we would assume the worst. The Soviets probably are capable of building 3000 or 4000 strategic delivery vehicles, and equipping their biggest rockets with as many as 40 separate hydrogen bombs. How would we know they hadn't done so? How would we know we shouldn't do the same? We wouldn't know.

Objections will be raised—indeed, they have been raised already—that the Soviets can't be trusted to keep their agreements, that the revolution in Iran has impaired our ability to check on Soviet compliance and that (regardless of the theoretical merits of SALT) the specific terms of the new agreement are disadvantageous to the United States and our allies. Dovish critics complain that the SALT II agreement doesn't really limit arms at all, but simply establishes new rules for arms-racing. And hawks charge that SALT, and the détente policy of which it is a part, serve to cloud the mind and sap the will of the West in the face of Soviet hegemonism. We take all these objections seriously, but we believe that the SALT treaty can survive them.

Let us begin with politics. We judge the Soviet Union to be an imperialist totalitarian state, a scourge of liberty and humane values everywhere, a menace to the West both militarily and politically. We judge that Soviet leaders, having advanced to their posts by stealth, guile and ruthlessness, are not to be trusted by people and nations who revere law and common decency. We look at Soviet gulags, death camps and psychiatric torture centers, and at Soviet barbarism in Czechoslovakia and Hungary and we have a picture of what the world would be like if the Soviet system prevailed. We do not doubt that if the Soviet Union could attain military superiority over the United States, it would try to exploit it, as it has exploited our post-Vietnam political vulnerabilities in Africa and the Middle East. We regard the Soviet Union as America's adversary—no, as our enemy. And yet, we do have a common interest in the survival of mankind. We do not believe that the Soviet leadership, however murderous, is suicidal. Sometimes it is said that the Soviets lost 20 million people in World War II, and that they might endure comparable casualties to control the world in World War III. But US nuclear power is capable of inflicting hundreds of millions of casualties, just as Soviet nuclear power could do in the United States. So we have a basis on which to talk, to limit nuclear weaponry and to establish a minimal level of understanding.

Verification: No Problem

Would the Soviets cheat on SALT if they could? We believe they would. If Soviet compliance were not subject to US verification, we would oppose the treaty. Loss of two electronic tracking stations in Iran does seem to have impaired somewhat the US ability to monitor Soviet missile tests, but administration officials say that we still have adequate ability to verify SALT using satellites, ground stations in Turkey and Alaska, spy ships at sea and intelligence aircraft. The Baltimore *Sun* . . . reported that without the Iran sites the US had successfully monitored two test firings of Soviet SS-18 missiles all the way from their launching at Tyuratam, in the southwest Soviet Union, to Kamchatka Peninsula on the Pacific coast. The Soviets have tried to encode the signals sent from their test missiles back to base —so-called "telemetry"—but the SALT agreement supposedly will prohibit any coding that impairs verification. American officials seem confident that the US could detect any attempt to cheat. The Soviets supposedly have exploited every possible loophole and ambiguity in earlier arms limitation agreements but they have not been found brazenly violating treaty terms. The strongest, most sophisticated opponents of SALT, including former deputy defense secretary Paul Nitze, do not regard the verification issue as decisive. Rather, it seems to be a refuge for senators who do not want to trouble themselves digging into the details of missile numerology. It is remotely possible that verification loopholes could be uncovered in the forthcoming debate. If they are, they should be closed. But the most serious objections to SALT do not lie here.

The most serious criticism of SALT is that it will place the US and its allies at a strategic disadvantage against the Soviet Union. Even though the agreement calls for both sides to have equal numbers of strategic launch vehicles, and even though the US has and will continue to have more nuclear warheads, Nitze and his allies argue that the crucial difference between the US and Soviet arsenals is in the payload of their land-based intercontinental ballistic missiles. In the 1960s, because of superior technology, the United States decided to build small, highly accurate ICBMs, whereas the Soviets, lacking US capabilities, built big, heavy missiles. The US pioneered in multiple, independently-targeted warheads (MIRV), and super accuracy. Each US Minuteman III ICBM contains three warheads; our Trident I submarine missiles have eight warheads and MX missiles, if we choose to build them, will have 10. Minuteman missiles can be fired thousands of miles and their warheads directed to land within 600 feet of their targets.

The Soviets still trail the US in miniaturization and accuracy. But Nitze's point is that by 1985 they will have caught up; and because their missiles are so much bigger than ours, they may have some 6200 warheads mounted on land-based ICBMs to our 2100. The importance of this is that, theoretically, the Soviet Union could fire one-third of its missiles at us, destroy all of our land-based missiles, and have two-thirds left in reserve to attack American cities in the event the United States retaliated with sea-based missiles, bombers or cruise missiles. Because of submarine and bomber advantages, the US currently has double the total warheads that the Soviets do; in 1985 we will have 12,000 compared to the Soviets' 8000. But SALT critics contend that the vulnerability of land-based ICBMs is decisive. If they were destroyed in a Soviet first strike, a US president would have to decide whether to attack Soviet cities, knowing US cities would be destroyed in return, or surrender.

Far-fetched Scenario

Actually, Nitze and others do not think matters would ever arrive at this pass. Rather, they say, the mere *perception* of Soviet ICBM superiority will be enough to cause the US to back away from confrontation in potential crises, to make the Soviets bolder and to cause third countries to lean toward the Soviet side. Coupled with acknowledged Soviet superiority in conventional weapons. SALT critics argue, this strategic advantage means that another Cuban missile crisis or a new Soviet threat to intervene in the Middle East would end in Soviet victory.

We find all this very far-fetched, but serious people take it seriously, and so we are forced to. We find it far-fetched to suppose that the Soviets could contemplate staging or threatening a simultaneous surgical surprise strike on 1000 US missile sites. How could they be sure all their missiles would work? How could they assume the US side could tell the difference, amid all the fireballs and dying, between a "surgical" attack on US missiles and a full-scale attack on the US? How could they be sure the president wouldn't order a massive retaliatory barrage before the Soviet missiles ever hit?

And yet, the fact is that US land-based missiles will become increasingly vulnerable to Soviet attack, at least theoretically, and the US, in prudence, is called upon to do something about it. But this does not require abandoning

SALT. It does not necessarily even require building MX missiles, which—with 10 warheads each—arguably would give the United States the same first-strike capability against Soviet land-based missiles that they might gain against ours. It does require that we be able to move and hide our missiles, so that the Soviets can't hit them. How to do this is being studied by the Pentagon, though the study is proceeding too slowly and is caught up in inter-service rivalry. Placing missiles on barges on the Great Lakes, coastal waters and inland waterways probably is the cheapest method, but what's important is for the administration to decide on one mobility arrangement and get on to building it.

There are three more major objections to SALT. One arises from a protocol lasting until the end of 1981 that is separate from the SALT treaty (which lasts through 1985), but also is legally binding. America's European allies, who favor SALT in general, are concerned that protocol restrictions on ground-based cruise missiles will be extended beyond 1981, thereby denying them the ability to develop this new unmanned-airplane technology for their own defense. The Soviet Union has a heavy advantage over NATO in so-called "theater" nuclear weapons and keeps adding to its arsenal. The New York *Times* reports that the Soviets are adding short-range SS-21 missiles to their formidable supply of intermediate-range SS-20s. Neither of these is covered by SALT. Soviet Backfire bombers, also excluded from the treaty (in a trade allowing us to build cruise missiles), may or may not be a strategic threat to the United States, but they certainly threaten Europe. It is important that the Carter administration give every assurance to our allies that they will be adequately protected—if not by negotiations leading to Soviet arms reductions, then by full development of air defenses, intermediate missiles, and cruise missiles. The US also must fulfill its obligations to modernize NATO conventional weapons. The Carter administration seriously faltered in its on-again, off-again mishandling of the neutron bomb decision. That weapon should be deployed to counter Soviet tank power, and the US must act in a way that will assure Europe that we understand the threat the Soviets pose.

Liberal Critics of SALT

Some SALT critics, led by Senator George McGovern, contend that the treaty doesn't limit arms at all, and that the Carter administration, to win ratification, has agreed to build enough new weapons to erase any arms control effects the treaty might have had. We can dispose of this quickly by asking McGovern to ask the Soviets why they refused to negotiate on the basis of President Carter's March 1977 "deep cuts" proposal, which would have made significant inroads in the arsenals on both sides. Also, we would point out that the new SALT agreement contains a nonbinding statement of principles calling for negotiations toward a permanent treaty that cuts back nuclear arms.

Some SALT opponents claim that the US should not conclude agreements with the Soviets when they are bent on world domination, when they encourage coups and Cuban interventions in Africa and the Middle East, and are expanding their naval and conventional military power worldwide. SALT, it is said, should be linked to Soviet good behavior elsewhere in the world. Obviously, there is a level of Soviet action—say, a cross-border invasion of another country—which would so seriously damage US-Soviet relations that we could not contemplate an arms agreement, when a return to the cold war would be appropriate. In the absence of that, however, we should combat Soviet interference with politics, foreign aid, diplomacy, persuasion— and, if necessary, covert action and even military action. The Senate should not defeat SALT because the Soviets are up to no good. It is *because* they are up to no good that we need SALT—to insure that we know what they are doing in the most dangerous area of our relationship.

LIMITED BUT SUBSTANTIAL ACHIEVEMENTS[5]

Pax Christi–USA and The Committee on the Present Danger are both opposing the ratification of SALT II. Pax Christi asserts that the treaty achieves too little; The Committee believes that the treaty is giving away too much. These two charges illustrate the vulnerability of the treaty. Two groups, with antithetical objectives, have formed a tactically identical position: defeat of SALT II.

Between these two positions it is possible to build a case of support for SALT II as a limited but necessary measure of arms control, deserving the support of all those, including Christians, who are committed to abolishing the nuclear threat to human life. The case has two dimensions: a general political-moral argument for SALT II; and a specific ecclesial discussion of the church and SALT II.

The *limits* of SALT II as an arms control measure are clear and should be clearly acknowledged. The procedural limits are rooted in the way these bilateral superpower negotiations are insulated from other actors in the international system. This isolation of the SALT process from other arms control or disarmament forums enhances the feeling among other states that the nuclear condominium, which could drastically impact them, is totally beyond their influence.

The substantive limits of SALT II are more significant. The actual reductions required by the treaty are marginal and the dynamic of development in key areas of weapons technology is not stringently constrained. Examples of substantive limits include the continuing development of weapons accuracy allowed by the treaty and the provision that

[5] From article entitled "Is SALT Worth Supporting? Yes," by Father J. Bryan Hehir, Associate Secretary of the Office of International Justice and Peace, United States Catholic Conference in Washington. *Commonweal.* 106:108–10. Mr. 2, '79. Copyright © 1979 Commonweal Publishing Co., Inc. Reprinted by permission.

each side will be allowed to produce and deploy one new missile during the life of the treaty. In terms of the numerical limits on missiles and warheads, the proposed ceilings are most often higher than present levels of development for either superpower. Critics of the treaty who charge that it achieves too little can legitimately indicate that it sanctions increased deployment of nuclear weapons for both sides. This litany of the limits of SALT II concentrates on the arguments of those who find it, in Bishop Gumbleton's words during a talk to Pax Christi's annual meeting in December, "a cruel hoax" rather than a step toward real disarmament. The full complexity of the SALT II debate can be understood, however, only when it is recognized that an entirely different range of criticisms against SALT II is based on the tendency, in Paul Nitze's words, "to subordinate security policies to hopes for advancing arms control rather than shaping arms control policies to our security needs."

Maintaining the SALT Process

It is clear that SALT II is limited; it is even more clear that it is *necessary*. It is necessary as an integral part of a process which is presently the only politically viable method of reversing the arms race. The key question is: what will defeat of SALT II do to ameliorate its limits? Is there any evidence that its defeat will produce more substantial forms of disarmament? Those opposing SALT II should reasonably be expected to answer this question. Those supporting SALT II must demonstrate its merits; the case rests on a convergence of arguments.

First, quantitative controls: the controls proposed by SALT II in terms of numbers of nuclear weapons are limited but not inconsequential. To evaluate them fairly requires that SALT be viewed as a process, with a history and a future. Arms control agreements are not an end in themselves; they must be interpreted in terms of their impact on a wider political context. SALT II does set new lower

limits on Strategic Nuclear Delivery Vehicles (SNDVs) —
bombers and missiles—and it does require destruction of
some SNDVs by the Soviet Union. The new limit of 2250
SNDVs, down from 2400, is higher than the present U.S.
development, but deeper cuts proposed early in the Carter
administration were rejected by the Soviets—understandably, given the nature of the proposal. The numbers are
not great, but in political terms it must be stressed that
this would amount to the first reduction of offensive weapons
in the history of the nuclear arms race. The political-psy-
chological significance of such a reduction should not be
lightly discarded either as a deception or a give-away. From
deterrence theory to debate about SALT II, psychology is
woven through the fabric of the debate. The impact of
negotiating the first reduction in three decades breaks the
mind-set that the technological dynamic is beyond political
control.

Second, the terms of SALT II are not only about quantitative controls. Unlike SALT I, which left the crucially important problem of multiple independently-targeted re-
entry vehicles (MIRVs) unresolved, SALT II devotes considerable attention to qualitative controls. The principal
method of control is the establishment of a series of sub-
ceilings under the 2250 SNDVs which restrict development
of various types of weapons systems. The limits on MIRVed
weapons remain at 1320; but within this category the accurate and powerful land-based MIRVed missiles are limited to 820. The numerical limits are still high, but the
central fact is the *principle* of qualitative control which can
in turn yield further reductions within the SALT process.

Third, there stands the ominous threat of what can be
expected if SALT II controls are not imposed. The arms
race is generated by a quasi-independent technological dynamic. The primary significance of the SALT process, as
part of a wider disarmament picture, is the chance to impose political control on the most powerful and dangerous
dimension of the technological revolution in this century.

It is necessary to ask those who would withhold support of SALT II because it is too limited what alternative forms of control they propose. The arms race is principally in the hands of states; we are left, for the foreseeable future, with limits to which states will agree. SALT II falls in that category, and should be evaluated in light of the projections now made about the future devoid of SALT II controls.

If SALT II fails there will be no existing framework for superpower arms limitation. The SALT I Interim Agreement on offensive weapons has expired. The ceiling of 2400 SNDVs will no longer hold, and careful estimates predict 3000 SNDVs by the mid-1980s. Since no qualitative controls will exist, MIRV production will be unconstrained both in terms of the number of MIRVed missiles and the number of warheads per missile. Politically, the failure of SALT II will inevitably be seen in the short term as a signal that the impetus for super-power arms control is dormant or dead. No attempt will be made here to predict what will happen on the Soviet side after the centerpiece of its foreign policy has collapsed. On the U.S. side, past experience illustrates that all candidates for new weapons systems will become actual contenders: the B-1, Trident II, along with MX will be on the legislative assembly line. Each system has its supporters within Defense and/or Congress; SALT II holds out the possibility of systemic control of the development and procurement process. Without SALT II, each weapons system becomes the subject of a "great debate" similar to the B-1 decision.

Fourthly, one must ask whether there is any evidence that the defeat of SALT II will contribute anything to the wider process of disarmament. There is a broader agenda than SALT II, but it is highly doubtful that much will occur in other forums without a SALT agreement. The Comprehensive Test Ban Treaty and the Mutual Balanced Force Reductions both involve the U.S. and USSR as central actors; it is difficult to believe they will survive the recriminations of a SALT II failure. The Nonproliferation

Treaty and its subsequent regime of constraints on nonnuclear states has been predicated from its inception on paragraph VI which pledges the superpowers to a meaningful
process of arms control. The restraints in horizontal proliferation are already fragile; they will be eroded by another
superpower failure on vertical proliferation.

Moral Value of SALT II

The political-moral case for SALT II is cast in terms of
these arguments: the key moral value is control; the political method is negotiated limitation among states. One can
argue both dimensions in reasonable fashion, but like all
political and moral arguments it is an appeal to reason, not
an infallible case. A new dimension enters the debate about
the treaty when we examine whether Christians should
support SALT II. Christians bring perspectives to the
debate which do not fit nicely into conventional political
discourse. It is possible, therefore, that a reasonable political-moral argument is at best interesting to them but not
compelling. Some comments, therefore, are in order about
Christians, the church and SALT II.

First, the controlling text in the discussion should be
from *The Pastoral Constitution on the Church in the Modern World:* "it happens rather frequently, and legitimately
so, that with equal sincerity some of the faithful will dis-
agree with others on a given matter." The text should
forestall quick conclusions that a given position is *the*
Catholic position on SALT. In the SALT debate, the technical data are sufficiently complex and moral analysis sufficiently controverted that there is room for more than one
Christian insight.

Second, the debate within the Catholic community,
given impetus by Pax Christi, is surely to be welcomed. At
the same time it is necessary to keep the Catholic debate in
focus. It is important for the participants, but it would be
a delusion to think the public debate about SALT will be
cast in terms of this exchange. Christians have an oppor-

tunity to participate in public policy debate, but they seldom can define the terms of the debate. That debate will be argued in terms of whether SALT II "gives away too much," not by whether "it achieves too little."

Third, even if we do not define the terms of the debate, we can determine our own position by criteria which are specific to our religious vision. The question, then, is whether the limited but substantial achievements of SALT II are compelling for the Christian conscience. Sorting out the answer requires further distinctions. In the first instance, it is clear that any SALT II agreement would rest upon the foundation of the strategic "balance of terror." But no arms control agreement is conceivable today which does not rest upon the deterrence relationship. In the second place, for guidance one can examine recent statements of the teaching church from *Peace on Earth* (1963) to Paul VI's *Address to the U.N. Special Session on Disarmament* (1978). These documents condemn the arms race unreservedly, yet woven through these statements is a theme which recognizes the complexity of moving from condemnations to constructive political change. This theme speaks of reversing the arms race in terms of "progressive disarmament," with stockpiles being reduced "equally and simultaneously," in a controlled process which yields security at least equal to the present situation. The purpose of these citations is simply to say that there is an existent rationale for Catholic support of measures that seek a limited form of control of weapons systems.

Fourth, in determining what position Catholics should take in the face of SALT II, it is helpful to use the traditional categories of an ethic of intention and an ethic of consequences. The intent of opposing SALT II because it is too limited may range from a determination to offer a distinct form of Christian witness to a decision to provide a counterweight against groups opposing the treaty as a giveaway. Intention is important in political ethics, but never solely decisive. The consequences must be coldly confronted: do we want to contribute to the failure of SALT II? Is it necessary to oppose SALT II in order to specify its limits? It seems there must be a way to continue the examination of the inadequacies of SALT II without being part of the coalition which seriously threatens to defeat it not in the name of disarmament, but in pursuit of escalation.

Pursuing a Larger Vision

Finally, there is embedded in the Catholic debate a larger ecclesiological question about the church's role in society. There is a form of Christian witness against war which refuses to take the conventional categories of political and ethical discourse as the means of determining Christian obligation. This position defined as "sectarian" (in an analytical not a pejorative sense) finds a useful form of witness in rejecting standard categories as a means of stating the war and peace issues. The contrary position, "the church model," brings its own categories to the societal debate but consciously tries to relate to and to inform the wider debate with insights of faith and reason drawn from the Christian tradition.

The dimensions and dangers of the nuclear age have moved an increasing number of Christians to a sectarian position, ethically and ecclesiologically, as the only viable ground on which to stand. If one can judge by statements of the last fifteen years, the teaching church has not moved to that posture. The argument of this article is that SALT II does not provide grounds for the institutional church to become sectarian in an ecclesiological or ethical sense. It should be sufficiently pluralist to shelter sectarian options in the community without itself adopting a sectarian view.

The refusal to take a sectarian stance will leave the church "in the middle" of the SALT II debate. In the face of criticisms that the treaty is "too little" or "too much" the middle position asserts that SALT II is not enough, but it is imperative as a step in a process. As usual the middle position is neither as clear nor as dramatic as the edges of an argument can be. It sacrifices clarity to complexity and often must blend commitment with compromise. But the middle is often where one can mesh the possible and the necessary in the policy process. This position supports what is presently possible in pursuit of a larger vision of what must be made possible.

III. AGAINST SALT II

EDITOR'S INTRODUCTION

The arguments of those who oppose SALT II center on opposite premises: those who regard it as a threat to U.S. security interests and diplomatic influence, and those who feel that it is a morally and politically inadequate expression of American policy on world disarmament. The view that SALT II will undermine U.S. military strength and security requirements, as in past agreements, is set forth at length in the initial article by Eugene V. Rostow, a Yale law professor writing in *Commentary*. "If," he projects, "mesmerized by old illusions about disarmament and new ones about détente, we accept the treaty, we will be taking not a step toward peace but a leap toward the day when a President of the United States will have to choose between the surrender of vital national interests and nuclear holocaust. No President should ever be put in such a corner."

The other side of the opposition to SALT II is set forth in the next article by Robert C. Johansen in *Harper's* Magazine. His plea for arms reduction rather than management reads in part as follows: "An understanding of the political context surrounding the entire SALT process reveals that it discourages a halt to the growth of armaments. Military and civilian officials in the Pentagon understand this, which explains, perhaps, why they will endorse the SALT treaty."

This anti-military stance is reinforced by the religious view of a Catholic theologian, writing in *Commonweal*, in the third article in this section. "Instead of emphasizing that the arms race has brought us to the most dangerous point of insecurity for all nations that the world has ever known," writes Bishop Gumbleton, "our political leaders are still trying to convince us that we can have security and peace through nuclear arms. The arguments made for the treaty strongly emphasize that we are not lessening in any way our dependency on nuclear weapons."

In the final article in this section, a senior fellow at the Brookings Institution speculates on what will happen if the accords reached in SALT II break down. He anticipates little change in either budget or programs in the relentless competition in arms that will go on, much as it did during détente.

THE CASE AGAINST SALT II[1]

In human disputation justice is only agreed on when the necessity is equal; whereas they that have the odds of power exact as much as they can, and the weak yield to such conditions as they can get.

      —THUCYDIDES, *History of the Peloponnesian War*

Over the last century, the yearning for peace has given rise—especially in Great Britain, the United States, Scandinavia, the Netherlands, and Canada—to the belief that disarmament agreements, or agreements for arms limitation, are an important means for securing peace. It would be more accurate to say that settled expectations of peace between nations result in disarmament. When neighbors share the same goals, agreements on arms limitation or disarmament can be of marginal utility. For example, the celebrated agreement between Great Britain and the United States providing that no warships be stationed in the Great Lakes has become the symbol for the general policy of Canada and the United States with respect to their common border. And many countries have had unarmed borders

---

[1] Article by Eugene V. Rostow, Sterling Professor of Law at Yale and Chairman of the Executive Committee of the Committee on the Present Danger, and author of several books. *Commentary.* 67:23–32. F. '79. Reprinted from *Commentary*, February 1979, by permission; all rights reserved.

for years without benefit of a formal treaty. But the enthusiastic advocates of arms-limitation treaties tend to forget that such agreements cannot achieve their goals when some of the parties pursue quite different policies.

The arguments made for SALT II today are the same as those put forward on behalf of the Washington Naval Treaty of 1922 and the other arms-limitation and arms-reduction arrangements on which the Western governments lavished so much time, attention, and hope during the 20's and 30's. [See Part I—Ed.]

The Washington Naval Treaty and its progeny did not prevent Pearl Harbor. We, the British, and the French, lulled by the treaty, and hard-pressed in any event to find money for naval-building programs, let our navies slide. We did not build our full quotas or modernize our ships. The Japanese and later the Germans, on the other hand, took full advantage of their quotas. We should recall what the phrase "pocket battleship" meant. The pocket battleship, which the Japanese and the Germans used with such great effect in World War II, was a cruiser with the striking power of a battleship—a powerful modern man-of-war built within the tonnage limits of the treaty.

The post-World War I arms-limitation agreements—demilitarization of the Rhineland as well as the various naval agreements—failed to prevent World War II. Indeed, those agreements helped to bring on World War II, by reinforcing the blind and willful optimism of the West, thus inhibiting the possibility of military preparedness and diplomatic actions through which Britain and France could easily have deterred the war. Churchill never tired of pointing out that World War II should be called the "Unnecessary War," a war which Anglo-French diplomacy could have prevented.

Despite this melancholy history, we are told everywhere that the SALT II agreement now in the final stages of negotiation will be "politically stabilizing"; and that the breakdown of the SALT negotiations, or the rejection of the prospective treaty by the Senate, would "end détente," "bring back the cold war," increase the risk of nuclear and of conventional war, and revive "the arms race," which would cost us another $20, $70, or $100 billion.

Better Than Nothing?

Emotionally and politically, this is the strongest argument for ratification: that even a bad agreement with the Soviet Union is better than no agreement at all. The issue presented by SALT, Senator George McGovern has said, is that "the alternative to arms control and détente is the bankruptcy and death of civilization." And in a speech in London on December 9, Secretary of State Vance said that "without an agreement, our technological and economic strength would enable us to match any strategic buildup, but a good agreement can provide more security with lower risk and cost. And we recognize that without SALT, the strategic competition could infect the whole East-West political relationship, damaging the effort to create a less dangerous world which is at the heart of Western foreign policies." Since, however, we were infinitely more secure without an arms-limitation agreement during the period 1945–72 than we have been since, the logic of this argument is not immediately apparent.

The claim that a SALT II agreement would be politically stabilizing, and would foster Soviet-American cooperation in other areas, is just as empty. We have had the Interim Strategic Arms Limitation Agreement with the Soviet Union—SALT I—since 1972. Far from stabilizing world politics, the Interim Agreement has been an important structural feature of the most turbulent and dangerous period of the cold war (the period ironically known as "détente").

Thus, during the six-and-a-half years following President Nixon's trip to Moscow in 1972, we have endured a series of major Soviet offensives. First, the Soviet Union defaulted on its obligations as a guarantor of the peace agreements of 1973 in Indochina. These agreements, for which Mr. Kissinger received a Nobel Prize, were treated by the Soviet Union as scraps of paper. The final North Vietnamese invasions of South Vietnam in 1974 could never have taken place without Soviet equipment and other help. Then the Soviet Union, which had promised President Nixon to cooperate with him in seeking peace in the Middle East, violated those promises by supplying, planning, encouraging, and even participating in the Arab aggression against Israel of October 1973.

So far as the 1972 Interim Agreement itself is concerned, Secretary of State Rogers testified to the Senate that we had made a number of unilateral interpretations of the agreement and that we should regard any breach of these policies by the Soviet Union as a violation of the "spirit" of the treaty. All these unilateral interpretations of the agreement were violated by the Soviet Union. We did nothing about them.

But the ultimate absurdity is the claim that SALT II would limit or reduce either arms or arms expenditures. The one thing the 1972 Interim Agreement on Offensive Strategic Arms did *not* do was to limit Soviet arms development or expenditure, or the growth of the Soviet nuclear arsenal.

The SALT I Interim Agreement was presented to Congress and the country with fanfares from President Nixon, Secretary of Defense Laird, and Mr. Kissinger, as he then was. We were assured that the agreement would slow down the Soviet buildup of strategic offensive weapons; discourage the Soviets from adopting counterforce strategies; and enhance peace and our security in other unspecified ways. But the principal claim made for the agreement was that it would apply "brakes to the momentum of Soviet strategic missile deployments," in Secretary Laird's words.

Yet instead of stabilizing or reducing its strategic offensive strength during the period of the Interim Agreement, the Soviet Union has moved ahead rapidly: far more rapidly, in fact, than had been predicted as possible by American intelligence. It has successfully MIRVed (that is, placed several warheads on a single missile) its ICBM (intercontinental ballistic missile) forces, taking advantage of their greater delivery capacity (throw-weight) to develop missiles with as many as 10 warheads per missile, as compared with 3 on our Minuteman III missile. It has improved the accuracy of its missiles and developed new and improved missiles to replace older ones within its forces. One of the most significant of these developments is the Soviet production of mobile ICBM's. President Carter has said that the Soviet Union has actually deployed mobile ICBM's. Whether or not this has happened to a significant extent, the experts agree that the Soviet Union could do so quickly and on a large scale. Mobile ICBM's would completely alter the nuclear equation, making ICBM's almost as elusive as submarines, and making it impossible, or much more difficult, to target a nuclear strike against them. The Soviet Union has also adopted "cold-launch" methods which permit a greater throw-weight with a given missile, and the more rapid reloading of the launcher after use.

Comparison of American and Soviet Strength

As a result of these changes, the Soviet strategic nuclear force has been radically enlarged since 1972 in all categories and, according to present estimates, will be far stronger by the early 1980s. At the time of the Interim Agreement, the aggregate throw-weight of the Soviet ICBM's was twice that of the American force. In the early 1980s, it will be about four times as large. The throw-weight of our own ICBM's is unchanged, and is not expected to change during the treaty period.

The Soviet Union is believed to have had 1,600 warheads available to its ICBM force in 1972, compared to our 2,154. In the early 1980s, we shall have the same number, 2,154, but the Soviet figure will rise to between 6,500 and 9,200, even under the limitations expected in a SALT II treaty. The Soviet Union is producing between 150 and 200 ICBM's a year. We make none. The area-destructive power of Soviet warheads will increase by a half; ours by an eighth. The capability of Soviet weapons to knock out hardened (defended) targets, such as missile silos, will have increased tenfold. If our cruise missiles, now under development, fulfill present expectations, ours will have increased fourfold.

In the category of submarines, the Soviets are believed to have had 845 SLBM's (submarine-launched ballistic missiles) at the time of the 1972 agreement, and presently are near the ceiling of 950. Some Soviet SLBM's are as large or larger than our Trident I, which we have not yet introduced. Our figure will not change. In warheads, we are believed still to have a substantial lead. In 1972 we had about 3,000 SLBM warheads; our present figure of 5,400 is not expected to change during the next few years—while it is anticipated that the Soviet figure of 845 will increase some fivefold as they MIRV their SLBM's.

The comparison of bomber forces is more difficult, depending on whether so-called medium bombers are included. Our heavy bomber force, still based on the out-of-date B-52, is declining, and President Carter has canceled its replacement, the B-1. We had 450 heavy bombers in 1972 to 140 for the Soviet Union, which also had 1,100 "medium" bombers assigned to missions in Europe or Japan, but available for attacks against the United States as well. In addition, the Soviet Union has and is manufacturing a new bomber, the Backfire, two-thirds the size of the B-1. It is not to be counted under the limits established by SALT II, although the State Department concedes that it can be used for intercontinental missions. By 1985, the Soviet Union will have 300 to 400 Backfire bombers. We will have no comparable planes by 1985 beyond our less proficient and much less numerous FB-111's.

While it is difficult to compare the bomber strength of the two nations in the field of intercontinental strategic nuclear weapons, there can be no question about the steady decline of our bomber superiority, which was one of the key premises of the 1972 agreement. That decline is measured not only in the comparison of the planes themselves, but in the development of Soviet air defenses, which we have decided to ignore altogether. The Soviet Union has a large and widespread network of fighter planes deployed for air defense, thousands of SAM's and other anti-aircraft weapons, and at least one anti-ballistic-missile (ABM) system in operation. The Soviets have actively continued ABM research and development since 1972, and presumably would be able to deploy more units on short notice. These defensive measures would exact a heavy toll in the course of any attack, and therefore create doubt about the perceived deterrent effect of our bomber and missile forces.

In short, instead of applying "brakes to the momentum of Soviet strategic missile deployments," SALT I served to increase that momentum. On the United States, SALT I had the opposite effect. Lulled by the treaty—as well as by illusions about "overkill," and by the high hopes we had invested in détente—into thinking that the "arms race" was being brought under control, we allowed ourselves to fall behind in most relevant categories of military power: behind in production; behind in research and development; and behind in programming.

A Costly Agreement

As for the claim that a SALT II treaty will reduce the cost of our own defense programs, General George M. Seignious II, the new director of the Arms Control and Disarmament Agency, said on December 13, 1978 that the SALT II agreement, as it seemed likely to emerge, coupled with the further development of the Soviet nuclear arsenal made possible by the agreement, "is going to require additional money to modernize the strategic systems we have." In his final press conference on October 30, 1978, Paul Warnke, the outgoing director of the Arms Control and Disarmament Agency, said that while he believed SALT II would save us money, by restraining certain forms of Soviet expansion we should otherwise have to match, it was not possible to "point to some form of saving" that the treaty would accomplish. For by establishing certain quantitative limits, the treaty would shift Soviet efforts to the quest for qualitative superiority. The effort to match qualitative improvements, based on active research and the development of new technologies, is hardly more economical than the repetitive manufacture of old-model weapons.

Yet the proponents of SALT II claim that the failure to achieve or ratify the treaty would add as much as $100 billion to our defense budgets over a five-year period. Those figures of extra costs if the SALT negotiation fails, or if the Senate refuses to consent to the treaty, are just as fanciful as President Nixon's claims that he had ended the cold war and achieved "détente."

There is no case, then, for SALT II as a step toward peace. The record is clear that the first SALT agreement on the limitation of offensive strategic weapons contributed to an intensification, not a lessening, of tensions between the United States and the Soviet Union throughout the world. The rapid Soviet buildup of new and advanced strategic weapons under the agreement gave rise to charges of "deception," "breach of faith," and indeed of breach of the agreement. And the 1972 Interim Agreement gave the Soviet Union certain great and tangible advantages. For example, we halted the development of our ABM systems, in which we had a technological lead. They, as already noted, have continued their research and development in that important field. There is no reason to believe that the process of continued negotiation with the Soviet Union would change this pattern.

According to information now generally available, the SALT II agreement will consist of a Treaty, a Protocol, and a Statement of Principles. The Treaty would expire on December 31, 1985, the Protocol . . . in 1981. . . .   The

Statement of Principles concerns the agenda for the negotiations of SALT III and has no terminal date.

The key provision of the SALT II treaty is that each side would be permitted to have the same number of strategic nuclear launch vehicles—2,400 until a date in 1982, and then 2,250. Within this limit, there is a sublimit of 1,320 on the number of launchers carrying multiple independently-targeted reentry vehicles (MIRV's) — ICBM's, SLBM's, and aircraft equipped to carry air-launched cruise missiles (ALCM's) with a range greater than 600 kilometers. At this writing, there is still reported to be a dispute between the American and Soviet negotiators as to whether all armed cruise missiles should be covered, or only cruise missiles armed with nuclear weapons.

There are two further sublimits within the category of 1,320 MIRVed launchers: (1) a limit of 1,200 on the number of MIRVed ICBM launchers plus MIRVed SLBM launchers; and (2) a sub-limit of 820 on the number of MIRVed ICBM launchers. Within that limit of 820, the Soviet Union would be allowed to have a number of fixed modern large ballistic-missile launchers (MLBM) equal to their present force in this category, either 308 or 326. This force includes the formidable Soviet SS-18's, which we believe now carry up to 10 separate megaton-range warheads. The SS-18 and SS-19 are capable of destroying protected missile housings and command centers. The Soviet SS-18 force by itself could destroy more than 90 percent of our land-based missile force, which consists of 54 Titans, 450 Minuteman II's, and 550 Minuteman III's, at one blow. The United States now has no such weapons, and the treaty would deny the United States the right to build any during the treaty period.

The treaty contains a number of limits on the modification of existing ICBM's, primarily the rule that any test of an ICBM with more reentry vehicles (RV's) than had previously been tested will cause it to be classified as a "new type"; each side is limited to testing one "new-type"

ICBM during the treaty period. The United States has tested 3 RV's on Minuteman III and the Soviet Union has tested 4 RV's on the SS-17, 6 RV's on the SS-19, and 10 RV's on the SS-18. There may also be agreement that no "new-type" ICBM can have more RV's than the maximum already tested for existing ICBM's—10 per missile for the Soviet Union, 3 for the United States. A late rumor suggests that both sides may have the limit of 10. Because of the delays in our MX program, however, there is no possibility that the United States can deploy a "new-type" ICBM prior to the expiration of the treaty.

The Soviet Union has made great progress in fractionizing its missiles, including those targeted against Europe which do not come under the treaty. There is agreement that the treaty should establish a limit of 14 RV's per missile for submarine-launched missiles, and of 20 or 35 (not yet agreed) for the number of cruise missiles on a single aircraft.

United States B-52's and our 4 B-1 test aircraft, and Soviet Bisons and Bears are to be counted as heavy bombers for purposes of the treaty. The Soviet Backfire bomber, much discussed in the negotiations, will not be counted, although it is capable of reaching targets throughout the United States, and is being produced steadily.

The treaty does not attempt to limit the number of missiles or warheads which may be produced and stored. Any "reductions" in the Soviet-deployed nuclear force required by the treaty need not result in the destruction of the weapons, but only their transference to a warehouse.

Both sides have agreed that neither side will take any action which would circumvent the purposes of the agreement. This provision raises serious problems with regard to the possible transfer of cruise missiles or cruise-missile technology to our allies. Whether this question has been satisfactorily resolved in the negotiations is not now clear. Similarly, there is agreement that each side would refrain from interfering with the other side's national means of verification. Here, too, damaging controversies have already developed, particularly with regard to Soviet encoding of "telemetry," which would enable them to circumvent our monitoring devices.

The protocol would ban the flight testing or deployment of mobile ICBM's and air-to-ground missiles and the deployment of ground- and sea-launched cruise missiles with a greater range than 600 kilometers during a three-year period. At this time, the provisions with respect to ground- and sea-launched cruise missiles, of special concern to our NATO allies, are reported to be still in negotiation.

First Strike Advantage

The provisions of the prospective SALT II treaty are highly technical and are difficult for the layman to judge. But the treaty as a whole can be measured by the layman against our goal in the continuing process of negotiating agreements with the Soviet Union on nuclear arms. That goal is to guarantee a nuclear stalemate—that is, to keep nuclear weapons from being used or brandished in world politics. It is an altogether sound goal, which has been the lodestar of American policy since we proposed the Baruch Plan in the late 40s. The operative principle of both the SALT I Interim Agreement and SALT II, in the American view, is to prevent the development of a situation in which either side might be in a position to gain a great advantage by a first strike—an advantage so dazzling that political leaders might be tempted to seize it.

What, then, do the data suggest by way of an answer to the basic question of how the prospective SALT agreement would affect the adequacy of our second-strike capability?

In attempting to answer this question, we must first realize that the deck now consists almost entirely of Jokers. Nonetheless, the attempt must be made. In formulating an answer, we must consider the number and vulnerability of missiles and warheads, their accuracy, their ability to reach key targets, and the effects of active and passive defense programs on the vulnerability of Soviet targets of all kinds.

As mentioned previously, the Soviet Union is continuing to build and modernize its strategic nuclear missile force at an alarming rate—150 to 200 ICBM's a year, compared to a rate of zero for the United States; 6 ballistic-missile submarines a year, as compared to zero for the United States (1½ a year in the 1980s) ; and 30 to 50 intermediate- to long-range bombers a year, as compared to zero for the United States. The Soviet Union builds missiles of a far greater throw-weight than ours, and can therefore put more or larger MIRVed warheads on each missile than we can, so that even under the proposals we made in March 1977, it could have twice as many ICBM warheads of five times the individual yield of ours. The figures reported in current drafts of the treaty would be even less favorable. And to make matters worse, the Soviets have made rapid advances in catching up on our previous technological advantages in MIRVing, accuracy, and smaller RV's.

With these trends in mind, former Deputy Secretary of Defense, Paul Nitze, who helped negotiate SALT I, concludes that SALT II in its present form will leave the United States without a credibly adequate second-strike capability. In a speech on December 5, he said: "Over the past fifteen years it would not have profited either side to attack first. It would have required the use of more ICBM's by the attacking side than it could have destroyed. By the early 1980s, that situation will have changed. By that time, the Soviet Union may be in a position to destroy 90 percent of our ICBM's with an expenditure of only a third of its MIRVed ICBM's. Even if one assumes the survival of most of our bombers on alert and our submarines at sea, the residue at our command would be strategically outmatched by the Soviet Union's retained warmaking capability."

In its study, *Is America Becoming Number 2?: Current Trends in the U.S.-Soviet Military Balance,* released on

October 5, 1978, the Committee on the Present Danger adds:

We do not have to assume that the Soviet Union will actually attack U.S. strategic forces. The point is that they will have the capacity to *increase their advantage* with a counterforce first strike. After such a first strike, the United States would still have a capability for a second-strike retaliation against Soviet economic and political targets—in plain words, against their "hostage" cities and industrial centers. If Soviet civil defense failed, we could do "unacceptable damage" to them, but their forces held in reserve would still be greater than ours, and we have no effective civil (or air) defense. Their third-strike potential would make our second-strike less credible. It would leave the U.S. with a dangerously inadequate deterrent.

In presenting SALT II, the administration dismisses such concerns. Spokesmen for the administration concede that Soviet progress in strategic arms and particularly in ICBM's makes our own ICBM force vulnerable, and that our old bombers would have a hard time penetrating Soviet anti-aircraft defenses either to launch cruise missiles or to drop bombs. But, they say, we still have a great many MIRVed submarine-launched missiles, and therefore, perhaps, still an edge in the total number of warheads.

U.S. Advantage "Transient"

Yet our present substantial advantage in warheads is a transient one. The inherent flexibility afforded by large throw-weight Soviet ICBM's and the momentum of the Soviet MIRV program can soon erase the United States advantage in numbers of warheads (unless, that is, we shift gears promptly and on an adequate scale).

Secondly, our increasing reliance on submarine-launched missiles presents problems of its own. Such missiles are still notably less accurate than ICBM's, and therefore less capable of striking at the Soviet missile sites and other military targets than at hitting cities.

In August 1978, the U.S. Arms Control and Disarmament Agency attempted to dispel these doubts in a "dynamic" study of U.S. and Soviet strategic capability through the mid-1980s, and to escape from the logic of what it called "static" measures of the two strategic forces. The study does not measure the capacity of each side to destroy the other, but purports to calculate the capacity of Soviet and American strategic forces to destroy a hypothetical set of 1,500 "hard" (or defended) and 5,000 "soft" (i.e., undefended) targets. It thus assumes away the important disparities between the number and hardness of the targets in each country. The Soviet Union now has more hard targets than the United States, and is rapidly hardening soft targets, while we are standing still, even with regard to command-and-control centers. By the mid-1980s, the Soviet Union will have twice as many hard targets as the United States.

The ACDA study also makes unrealistic assumptions about the destructibility of soft targets as the result of the explosion of a single weapon, whatever its size and yield. It makes inadequate allowance for anti-aircraft and anti-missile defenses and the effect of Soviet civil-defense measures.

But there is a deeper problem with the ACDA analysis, which runs though the whole of the administration's case for SALT II. Our leaders tell us that the Soviet rulers will be restrained by their knowledge of our capability to inflict unacceptable damage on their people and their society if they push us too far.

However plausible this argument may have been up to the time of the Cuban missile crisis, when we still enjoyed overwhelming nuclear superiority, it has long since lost even the appearance of conviction. But Secretary of Defense Brown, Ambassador Paul Warnke, and other official spokesmen for the administration continue to repeat it as gospel. It remains the heart of their argument for SALT II. Indeed, for all practical purposes it is the whole of it.

I have always had the greatest difficulty in accepting this theory—Robert McNamara's theory of mutual assured destruction (MAD)—according to which we and the Soviets would hold each other's cities and people hostage, thus preventing any first strike, and neutralizing nuclear weapons. I find it hard to imagine that the President of the United States would actually order the destruction of Moscow or Leningrad, save under circumstances of the most extreme provocation, such as the actual prior destruction of major American cities. I find such a step nearly inconceivable if our major cities had not been destroyed, and the exchange would result in the immediate destruction of New York and Washington, even if our ICBM's had been destroyed. Secretary Brown's threat to blow up Soviet cities in retaliation for a Soviet first strike against our satellites or our ICBM's would be less than credible if the Soviets had enough weapons left in reserve to blow up our cities and possessed substantial enough reserves to dominate the postwar world. A Soviet arsenal of that size could neutralize our nuclear forces and emasculate our second-strike capability. It would thereby make us vulnerable to Soviet political coercion.

It is this analysis of the diminishing credibility of our threat to blow up the Soviet population which puts the argument of "overkill" into perspective. The possibility of using our submarine forces in an immediate strike against Soviet cities, always dubious, is now close to the margin of futility. The same cannot be said for the growing Soviet capacity to attack our ICBM's and other military targets. If we allow Soviet superiority to reach a certain level, the Soviets will have checkmated our threat to attack their soft targets.

In addition to its reliance on an increasingly dubious second-strike capability against cities and people, SALT II would inhibit us from reestablishing our second-strike capability against hardened military targets—in the current state of the nuclear balance, the retaliatory possibility which has the most credibility as a deterrent, and as an option for action if deterrence fails.

To deal with the threat of a Soviet first-strike capacity,

and to restore the strategic balance generally by the early 1980s, will not be easy. The President's decisions to cancel or delay the B-1 bomber, the MX missile, and the Trident submarine make it nearly impossible for those weapons to be available before the late 1980s, even assuming that the decisions against them are reversed. It probably would take nearly as long, and cost nearly as much, to deal with the problem in the short run by reviving the production of Minuteman III's (or B-52's). The Minuteman III production line has been closed recently. And a crash program along these lines, or its equivalent, would be prevented by the numerical ceilings established in SALT II.

At this time, it seems probable that the treaty would also prevent the United States from adopting the only feasible "quick fix" for dealing with the problem, the promising plan for deploying missiles using a multiple aim-point system (MAPS), the so-called "shell game." Under this proposal, the United States would construct a large number of vertical protective shelters or silos, each capable of holding an ICBM and its launcher. Some would be empty. The missiles would be moved periodically, to make a first-strike against them highly problematical. According to reports, the Soviet Union has rejected an American inquiry about the compatibility of this idea with the treaty.

These are the basic reasons why critics have said that SALT II would freeze us in a position of inferiority, and deny us an opportunity to redress the balance before the critical period of the early 1980s, when all the indices would have turned against us.

Doubts on Verification

As to the problem of verifiability, several thoughtful students of the subject have expressed the view that technological developments have by now made it altogether impossible to regulate nuclear arms by verifiable arms-control treaties. There is certainly merit in their contention. For example, what are politely called "national means of verification"—satellite photography and electronic sur-veillance, largely—cannot answer many of the questions posed by the newer technologies. And satellites themselves have become vulnerable, a development Paul Warnke has called "alarming." No camera can tell how many separate warheads are carried by a single missile, or measure its thrust, its accuracy, or the explosive power of the weapons it carries. Nor can it see or otherwise identify the missiles kept in warehouses or factories, although missiles can be fired from such locations as well as from launchers, and can be deployed quickly in crisis situations to change the equations of deterrence.

The administration was campaigning hard to sell the SALT treaty even before it was negotiated. That campaign has given rise to a large number of speeches, memoranda, and articles pleading the case for SALT II. Among them, Jan M. Lodal's recent piece [See Part II] is typical in outlook and more detailed than most in analysis. It invokes three of the same criteria for judgment used here: (1) that the treaty contribute to the stability of the strategic balance; (2) that it be verifiable by national means; and (3) that it not adversely affect the security of our allies. But Mr. Lodal seems to reach a different conclusion. I say "seems to reach" because his treatment of each issue supports a negative judgment on the treaty; nonetheless, at the end Mr. Lodal says that SALT II cannot "be opposed on its technical merits."

1. In contending that SALT II would contribute to stra-tegic stability, Mr. Lodal points to the fact that the treaty specifies an equal number of launchers for both sides. He does not consider the problem posed by the agreement not to include the Soviet Backfire bomber—which, as already mentioned, can be targeted against the entire United States —in the number of bombers permitted under the treaty. But more important, he ignores the fact that the treaty does not cover the manufacture and storage of missiles. As Paul Nitze has commented, "The basic currency of the negotia-

tions . . . became limits on the number of launchers, not limits on missiles and their characteristics." This, adds Nitze, "has proven to be the wrong currency." Obviously, no situation can be considered stable if it can be changed in hours by the movement of missiles from warehouses to launchers, some of which are already mobile, as Mr. Lodal himself notes.

Mr. Lodal concedes that by the early 1980s the Soviet Union will lead the United States by most measures of nuclear power. We will be ahead only in the relative number of warheads deployed—and that lead will be diminishing rapidly. And Mr. Lodal also admits the main point—that the Soviet Union will soon have the capacity to destroy our ICBM sites, airfields, and other military targets with a fraction of their ICBM force. He argues, however, that by the mid-1980s our air borne cruise missiles, if they are developed successfully, would significantly offset Soviet superiority in ICBM's and thus maintain stability. He does not consider the vulnerability of our bomber-cruise-missile system (based on the aging B-52) to various kinds of attack. In fact, he does not mention Soviet active defenses at all, nor does he consider their grave implications for stability.

Mr. Lodal's position would be that such vulnerabilities are not significant. His ultimate contention is that the possibility of retaliation against Soviet cities and other soft targets, using our submarine-launched missiles, assures strategic stability even in the face of the growth of the MIRVed Soviet ICBM force. He does not mention the disquieting reports, which have now become public, of Soviet gains in anti-submarine warfare.

He does, however, grant that the assumptions of the McNamara doctrine are now subject to "serious argument" and that no President would want to face a crisis with only the options of doing nothing or launching an all-out attack on Soviet cities. Nevertheless, that is exactly the position he accepts. He dismisses the bearing of Soviet civil-defense programs on strategic stability in a footnote, suggesting that we could substantially offset the Soviet advantages derived from their programs of civil defense by using a small number of heavier bombs with high radioactive fall-out—a most unattractive possibility, and totally inadequate to boot. And he even contends that after we have deployed cruise missiles and MX—it is hoped by the late 1980s—we could counter a Soviet threat by launching a counterforce first strike of our own. This is the course we refused to consider during the period of our nuclear monopoly. To suggest it now is the counsel of desperation.

Mr. Lodal concludes that unless the Soviet Union agrees early in the SALT III negotiations to significant reductions in land-based ICBM's, "the strategic balance in the mid-1980s is likely to be determined to a much greater extent by the force-deployment programs of the two sides than it is by the provisions of arms-control agreements." Since he also observes that the Soviet Union cannot be expected to make unilateral concessions simply because we have chosen to forgo certain programs of our own, it is difficult to see how Mr. Lodal's argument supports his conclusion that SALT II would contribute to strategic stability.

2. With regard to verification, Mr. Lodal's case is equally mystifying. He does not mention Secretary Brown's public warnings about the Soviet capacity to destroy our satellites. Nor does he mention missiles kept in reserve, which are not covered by the agreement and cannot be verified by national means.

Mr. Lodal takes at face value the provisions in the treaty purporting to limit the number of warheads on missiles and their throw-weights. But he admits that we could not verify compliance with such limits, unless the Soviets should agree to cooperative procedures for verification. As of this writing, they have not done so. Yet Mr. Lodal has confidence in the possibility of Soviet cooperation in verification. He bases this confidence on two instances of Soviet "cooperation"—their agreement to rules through which we might distinguish heavy bombers carrying weapons from those used as tankers; and the Soviet promise not to deploy intercontinental SS-16 ICBM's. The SS-16's are indistinguishable from SS-20's, the mobile, MIRVed, intermediate-range missiles now causing so much alarm in Europe. The S-20's can easily be converted into SS-16's by adding another stage. This gives the Soviet Union the capacity to break out of the limits of the treaty rapidly. It is hard therefore to understand Mr. Lodal's satisfaction in the Soviet "concession." It hardly makes the counting process verifiable by national means.

3. Mr. Lodal admits that European concern with the implications of SALT II for the defense of Europe is justified in view of the massive Soviet deployment of conventional and theater-nuclear arms (including chemical-warfare equipment) facing Europe. The answer, he says lamely, is that Europe must accept "the proposition that the 'nuclear umbrella' can go only so far in providing security for Europe," and that Europe must improve its conventional forces. And he hopes that the SALT III negotiations will correct the present NATO imbalance, assure European security, and prevent the decoupling of the alliance.

Given the nature of Soviet negotiating habits, it is hard to detect any basis for such hopes. If we could not prevent a weakening of our nuclear relation with Europe during the SALT II negotiations, how could we expect to do so during the SALT III negotiations, when our military position, and therefore our bargaining position, are expected to be weaker?

Defending U.S. Interests

The security implications of nuclear weapons, however, go far beyond the question of intercontinental nuclear exchanges between the United States and the Soviet Union, the subject to which SALT II is confined. The United States nuclear arsenal is the fulcrum on which the possibility of deterrence at every level depends. To change the metaphor, it is the center of a web of relationships which define the political as well as the military power of the United States. The SALT II treaty cannot be judged in isolation, because the universe of nuclear weapons is not a self-contained and disagreeable subject, isolated from the daily business of government. SALT II poses the ultimate question of national security, the connection between military power and political influence.

To repeat it once again, the goal of our nuclear weapons is to deter the use of, or the credible threat to use, nuclear arms in world politics. But the mission of our nuclear forces goes beyond making it too expensive for the Soviet Union to consider launching a nuclear attack against the United States. They must also provide a nuclear guarantee for our interests in many parts of the world, and make it possible for us to defend those interests by diplomacy or by the use of theater military forces whenever such action becomes necessary. The preceding sentence deserves underlining, for most people do not yet realize the many connections between the strategic nuclear balance, on the one hand, and ordinary diplomacy and the use of conventional and other theater forces in aid of diplomacy, on the other. Behind the shield of our second-strike capability, we carry on the foreign policy of a nation with global interests, and defend them if necessary by conventional means or theater forces.

Secretary of State Dulles tried to change this policy by announcing the doctrine of "massive retaliation." We should not fight protracted land wars, he said, in places chosen by the Soviet Union for confrontation, but use our nuclear power instead to strike at the Soviet Union, the source of the danger. It was an empty threat. In fighting border wars, where absolutely vital American interests were not at issue, we were unwilling to consider using nuclear weapons against the Soviet Union, even during the period of our nuclear superiority. This policy is rooted in our national character and the nature of our civilization. It will not change. Even where the defense of Europe is concerned, our reflex response to the change in the nuclear balance is to enlarge NATO conventional forces, to reduce the risk that nuclear weapons would have to be used in the event of a Soviet attack.

The Soviet doctrine with regard to the utility of nuclear weapons is quite different. As we are finally beginning to realize, the Soviets are not interested in mutual deterrence and nuclear stalemate. To the Soviets, clear nuclear superiority is the ultimate weapon of coercive diplomacy—the Queen of their chess set, through which they think they could achieve checkmate without having to fight either a nuclear or a conventional war.

Effective American nuclear deterrence alone cannot keep the Soviet Union from using conventional forces, at least against targets they think we regard as secondary, like Korea, Vietnam, or Ethiopia. In most such situations, except for massive attacks on our most vital interests, like Western Europe or Japan, defense has to be provided by conventional forces in the first instance. But the absence of effective American nuclear deterrence—that is, the erosion or neutralization of our second-strike capability—would deny all credibility to our *conventional*-force deterrent. No one would believe that we would send in the Marines if they could be counterattacked by locally superior Soviet or satellite troops and our second-strike capability was in doubt.

Need for Nuclear Credibility

The point is brought out by a quick review of our experience with the problem since 1945.

In the early postwar years, we had a monopoly of nuclear weapons. And for a decade or so after that—until the middle or late 60s—we had overwhelming nuclear superiority. Nonetheless, in that period we had to deal with a long series of Soviet-managed attacks on our interests, from the early threats to Iran, Greece, and Turkey to the Berlin airlift, the war in Korea, the Cuban missile crisis, the war in Indochina, and the recurrent crises in the Middle East and Africa.

We dealt with those threats by diplomacy or, when diplomacy failed, by the use of, or the credible threat to use, conventional forces. But the nuclear weapon was always the decisive factor in the background. During the Berlin airlift, the shadow of our nuclear monopoly kept the Soviets from firing on the allied planes, and then persuaded the Soviet Union to end the blockade. The exercise had too many uncertainties and had become too risky, so the Soviet Union gave it up.

The essence of the problem is illustrated by the Cuban missile crisis of 1962. There, the Soviet Union secretly undertook to introduce land-based nuclear missiles into Cuba, in violation of their assurances to us, and in the face of private and public warnings from the President of the United States. Such action would have altered the basic equation of nuclear deterrence, and gravely affected the credibility and effectiveness of American diplomatic warnings to the Soviet Union. At that time, we had unchallengeable nuclear superiority. If there had been a nuclear exchange, the Soviet Union would have suffered about 100 million casualties and the United States 10 million. We had equally obvious conventional-force superiority in the area. If we had invaded Cuba, the Soviet Union could not have opposed the invasion effectively with either conventional or nuclear forces. By mobilizing an invasion force in Florida and instituting a limited naval blockade of Cuba, we demonstrated our will to insist on the evacuation of the Soviet missiles from Cuba, at a minimum. Confronted by these realities, the Soviet Union backed down.

Since the late 50s, the Soviet Union has been engaged in a massive military buildup, both in nuclear and conventional forces, designed to reverse the relationships which determined the outcome of the Berlin airlift, the Korean war, and the Cuban missile crisis. It is a buildup without

parallel in modern history. Over the last sixteen years it
has been proceeding steadily at a rate of at least 4 percent
to 5 percent a year in real terms. In strategic weapons, the
rate of increase has been at least 8 percent a year. Increases
compounded at the rate of 5 percent or 8 percent a year
over so long a period make the Soviet military establishment formidable and sinister.

The first result of this Soviet buildup was evident in
Vietnam. In the late 60s and early 70s, our nuclear superiority was no longer so evident as it had been at the time of
the Cuban missile crisis; indeed, superiority had given way
to stalemate. The deterioration of our nuclear advantage
led to the erosion of our position and profoundly affected
the final stages of the conflict.

There can be no question that since Vietnam our nuclear position has slipped from stalemate to the borders of
inferiority. While the experts argue about whether we are
already inferior to the Soviet Union in overall nuclear
power, they are agreed that if present trends continue we
shall be significantly inferior—and soon. Some careful studies
contend that the strategic force relationships which dominated the Cuban missile crisis will soon be reversed, unless
we undertake a crash program immediately—that in the
event of a nuclear exchange we should risk 100 million
casualties and the Soviet Union 10 million. Even if the
figure were 100 to 20 or 30, it is not difficult to anticipate
what would happen if we were to allow such a situation to
develop. A perceptive student of the problem has remarked
that, confronting such a scenario, even General Curtis Le-
May would advise "accommodation." Our foreign policy
and our conventional forces would be impotent, and we
would acquiesce.

It is the first objective of Soviet policy to achieve such a
situation. This—not nuclear war itself—is what our nuclear-
weapons program and the SALT negotiations are all about.
The Soviets have prolonged the negotiations over SALT II

as long as possible—just as Hitler prolonged arms-control negotiations in the 30s—since we continue to mark time in our own military and political programs during SALT negotiations, and obligingly make decisions, like the cancellation of B-1, the postponement of MX and Trident, and the deferring of the enhanced-radiation warhead (the so-called neutron bomb), in the vain hope of inducing similar restraint on the Soviet side. The Soviets view SALT II as a major instrument for lulling American anxieties until it is too late to do anything to reduce them. Meanwhile, they move rapidly and effectively to seize control of the entire Persian Gulf area in the belief that such a position would permit them to bring Europe, Japan, and the Arab world to their knees because the United States would not have the usable military power to oppose it.

Many tend to dismiss the vision of nuclear war as unthinkable. But the vision of Soviet political coercion, backed by overwhelming nuclear and conventional forces, is so far from unthinkable as to have become a likely possibility, thanks to the drift of American foreign and defense policy in the post-Vietnam period.

Context for a Decision

The debate over ratification of the SALT II treaty requires Congress and the American people to pass judgment on that policy as a whole. It is the only context in which the problem of nuclear arms becomes intelligible.

At the present time our foreign and defense policy is rich in contradictions. On the one hand, the President says that all our security treaties will be honored as in our national interest. On the other hand, he refuses to ask for the naval forces which would be necessary to fulfill those treaties, in view of the size of the Soviet navy and other military forces, and the nature of the Soviet Union's policy of indefinite expansion into the military vacuums of world politics. There are many other such paradoxes—the withdrawal of our ground forces from Korea, for example. Does that step mean that the President is prepared to use nuclear weapons if necessary to stop an attack on an area vital to the security of Japan? The list could be extended indefinitely, from our refusal to cooperate in the restoration of a stable monetary system to the passivity of our response to Soviet actions in Africa and the Persian Gulf area.

The actions and vocabulary of the Carter administration in the field of foreign and defense policy derive from two entirely different conceptions of the national interest. On the one hand, many cling to the 19th-century isolationist view, given new life (and a new rhetoric) by the Vietnam catastrophe, that the United States can be safe, perhaps with our Western European friends, as a small, rich, industrialized enclave in a world dominated by hostile forces. The major premise of the alternative theory, which has dominated our foreign policy from Truman's day, is that the United States can continue to develop as a free and open society only in a stable world order, a world of wide horizons, in which aggression is prevented, or defeated when it occurs, by collective security and other arrangements of collective defense; a world in which political, social, and economic progress is sought by international cooperation; and one in which the United States necessarily plays a full and responsible part.

These two conceptions of American foreign policy cannot be reconciled or compromised.

Thus far, however, President Carter has refused to choose between them. In recent months, his words have sounded more Trumanesque, but his actions have remained McGovernite. Many believe that a clear choice would revive the divisions in the nation, particularly in the Democratic party, which exploded with such force during the final stages of the Vietnam war. The President has preferred to let sleeping dogs lie.

That comfortable posture has become impossible. The

pressures of Soviet policy at a dozen points around the world, most particularly the bold Soviet thrust in the Persian Gulf region, would make it suicidal to continue on such a course. Yet the SALT II agreement, coupled with our continued retreats and withdrawals, and the inadequacy of our military programs, would also make it nearly impossible for us to restore and stabilize the world balance of power on which our safety as a nation depends.

Some experts in the field assume that we must accept SALT II despite its potential for condemning us to strategic inferiority, because the American people are unwilling to take "the giant strides forward" which would be required to assure nuclear parity and to maintain a credible and usable second-strike capacity. This defeatism is altogether unwarranted. The American people will spend and do whatever is required to assure the safety of the nation, if their leaders tell them the truth, as President Truman did, and explain the central importance of nuclear weapons to our security and to the foreign policies we employ to protect it.

Because the debate over SALT II presents a unique opportunity for telling this truth, it may well become a major turning-point for the future. If, mesmerized by old illusions about disarmament and new ones about détente, we accept the treaty, we will be taking not a step toward peace but a leap toward the day when a President of the United States will have to choose between the surrender of vital national interests and nuclear holocaust. No President should ever be put into such a corner. But if, overcoming these illusions, we permit ourselves to see the SALT II treaty for what it truly is—an expression of American acquiescence in the Soviet drive for overwhelming military superiority—we will give ourselves a last chance to restore the strategic balance that is the only guarantee of peace in the nuclear age and the only context in which the survival of our civilization and its values can be safely assured.

SALT WAS NEVER INTENDED TO DISARM[2]

Although I have spent most of my time in recent years trying to halt the arms buildup, I cannot in good conscience join the campaign to ratify the new treaty emerging from the Strategic Arms Limitation Talks (SALT II). An understanding of the political context surrounding the entire SALT process reveals that it discourages a halt to the growth of armaments. Military and civilian officials in the Pentagon understand this, which explains, perhaps, why they will endorse the SALT II treaty. Although the treaty does not dictate an increase in armaments, the negotiation and ratification processes provide the political conditions for an increase in military expenditures and overall destructive capability. Thus, I doubt that the provisions of the SALT II treaty are desirable enough that individuals and groups who want to reverse the arms race should devote their time, energy, and money to ratification.

To be sure, if we look only at the SALT II treaty itself, it might seem that we would be better off with it than without it. But that conclusion is a product of short memories and ignorance of the events surrounding the treaty, and forgotten is the intention, abandoned after SALT I, of achieving a treaty of unlimited duration. (SALT II will last until 1985.) It is also forgotten how much lower was the number of warheads, how much more stable was the strategic doctrine, how much less capable the superpowers were of fighting a nuclear war when SALT began than they are today. If one measures from the beginning of SALT

[2] Article entitled "Arms Bazaar: SALT Was Never Intended to Disarm," by Robert C. Johansen, president of the Institute for World Order and author of *The National Interest and the Human Interest: A Normative Analysis of U.S. Foreign Policy. Harper's.* 258:21-9. My. '79. Copyright © 1979 by Harper's Magazine. All rights reserved. Reprinted from the May 1979 issue by special permission.

in 1969, it is hard to believe that arms opponents would be in any worse position if there had been no SALT at all. SALT helped to make multiple warheads (or MIRVs: multiple independently targetable reentry vehicles) acceptable, and now it is giving a boost to the cruise missile, the M-X (a mobile missile), and the shift to a nuclear war-fighting capability, as opposed to a posture aimed simply at deterring an attack. Since SALT I was signed, the United States has deployed roughly 4,000 of the 10,000 warheads in its strategic arsenal. The achievement of both SALT I and SALT II is to curtail relatively insignificant parts of a quantitative arms race so that more money and brainpower can be devoted to a significantly more dangerous qualitative arms race.

The value of SALT is also miscalculated because political leaders are eager to attribute historic importance to their work—an importance that history often later belies. SALT II is based on slightly revised missile ceilings agreed upon by President Ford and Soviet President Leonid Brezhnev at Vladivostok more than four years ago. Ford described the Vladivostok Accord as "a real break-through that puts a cap on the arms race, . . . thus preventing an arms race with all its terror, instability, war-breeding tension, and economic waste." Secretary of State Henry Kissinger observed that when the accord was formally ratified, this "major breakthrough [would] be seen as one of the turning points in the history of the post–World War II arms race." More than four years have passed, and the Vladivostok ceilings have not been significantly exceeded by either side. Nonetheless, no evidence supports the contention that a major breakthrough has occurred in putting a cap on the arms buildup. Indeed, now that he is no longer Secretary of State, Kissinger seemed to possess a steadier grasp of the facts when he said recently that the SALT II treaty "at best slightly limits existing weapons programs."

SALT as Charade

SALT is more a charade than an arms reversal program. It serves the political needs of politicians, not the security needs of the human race. Leaders act as if they are making something big happen, but progress is recorded only in the military budget and in destructive capability. Weighty Senators, whether they be Henry Jackson seeking to expand his power in the Democratic party or Howard Baker and other Republican Presidential apprentices, appear on the political stage as actors exercising seasoned judgment and cautious wisdom by suggesting that they might oppose ratification because SALT II would restrict the United States too much. Always eager for drama, the media eagerly pick up an impending battle on Capitol Hill, make it newsworthy, and describe mere political theater as vital to the future of the Republic—meanwhile ignoring what is significant about the public's loss of control over the militarization of the planet.

Not all of these people understand that they participate in a charade, but neither do they seriously question how present military policies, with or without SALT, will increase human security in the long run. The quality of the charade is illustrated by the President's strategy of trying to increase the number of Senatorial votes for SALT II ratification by appointing a career military officer, George Seignious, to head the Arms Control and Disarmament Agency. If the Washington climate is so hostile to arms reductions that a military official and previous opponent of arms control must head the agency responsible for reductions in order to get Senate ratification of a treaty as harmless to the military as SALT II, can anyone really believe that we are about to take a significant step down the road toward arms reductions?

The greatest threats to peace by arms competition today are the qualitative improvements that make weapons faster, more deadly, more accurate, and more difficult to detect or defend against. SALT II will not prevent a single impor- tant qualitative development now on the drawing boards.

Proponents of SALT II, whether in Moscow or Wash- ington, point out that SALT II is desirable because it will contribute to détente. That may or may not be true, but we should recall that military expenditures, even after dis- counting inflation, have risen faster during détente than previously. SALT II will not scale down the diplomatic advantages the two military giants enjoy in their relations with other countries—advantages derived in part from their military power. As a result, other governments will con- tinue to feel the need for more arms if they seek to reduce inequities in global decision-making.

Détente and the SALT agreement between the United States and the Soviet Union signal not an end to arms com- petition, but instead an accord between the two most heav- ily armed governments on how to manage the undiminished arms competition. SALT II is a clever managing device to enable the United States and the Soviet Union to put fewer resources into the type of weapons—stationary, land-based, single-warhead ICBMs (intercontinental ballistic missiles) —in which an increase in their superiority over the rest of the world's governments will no longer matter. Moscow and Washington will then pour more money and brain- power into areas of technology where they can further out- pace the rest of the world militarily.

Even with the promise of successful negotiations, the Carter Administration has already projected for the next several years an average annual increase in military ex- penditures of 3 percent above inflation. In sharp contrast to his campaign pledge of a $5–$7 billion cut in the military budget, President Carter recently declared: "Our goal . . . is to increase the real level of defense expenditures. This is our goal." Increased spending by the United States and the Soviet Union will be used in part to develop and produce advanced nuclear warheads and delivery systems.

When the number of strategic missiles was limited by

SALT I seven years ago, Defense Department officials used this limit as an argument for putting more than one warhead on each missile. This technological "improvement," when later imitated by the Soviet Union, produced new Soviet capability that now makes the U.S. ICBM force vulnerable to Soviet attack and therefore becomes the excuse in the United States for a new mobile ICBM, the M-X. Pentagon officials also agreed to support SALT I on condition that they could develop the cruise missile, which was not covered by SALT I. The cruise missile, paradoxically, is a stumbling block in negotiating a SALT II agreement, and it will make extremely difficult the inspection of any future effort at limitation.

SALT'S "Guiding Principle"

When SALT II established a ceiling of 1,320 MIRVs at the 1974 Vladivostok meeting of President Ford and Soviet President Brezhnev, this high missile ceiling quickly became a target for large additional deployments. At the time the U.S. had deployed 832 missiles with multiple warheads. The Soviet Union had none. That historical moment presented an easy opportunity to have MIRVs banned completely, but they were not, because of the guiding principle for arms-control negotiations: limit the weapons considered least important to develop, and allow unrestricted development in other areas.

SALT II negotiators have carefully followed this principle. The treaty will allow the further testing of a MaRV (maneuverable reentry vehicle) to increase warhead accuracy. This is useful primarily for attacking an opponent's nuclear forces and for establishing a nuclear war–fighting capability. Such targeting precision is not necessary for simple deterrence of an attack. It will, however, stimulate a response from the Soviet Union, which will then make the U.S. deterrent more vulnerable and therefore will be used as the rationale for new U.S. deployments. The high MIRV ceiling in SALT II, for example, is already being used to justify the need for the M-X. Few people recall that the earlier U.S. arms-control decision not to try to ban MIRVs is now the stimulant for an entirely new ICBM.

U.S. negotiators in SALT II protected the right to develop the M-X, a larger, more accurate missile, with the intention of making it mobile so as to keep the Soviet Union guessing where it is stationed. Because of its multiple warhead capability, this missile will increase the threat to Soviet land-based missiles, make Soviet leaders more uneasy during a crisis, and stimulate them to match new U.S. technology. It will also make inspection of any future limitations much more difficult, thus decreasing the prospects for genuine strategic reductions if there should ever be a SALT III treaty. The decision to develop this new missile became a foregone conclusion as the negotiations proceeded, not because there was a security need for it, but because a payoff was needed for Pentagon officials to get their support for SALT II. Thus, the more arms-control negotiations appear to be serious and successful, the more rapidly the normal resistance to unnecessary new arms programs erodes, which is why "success at SALT" has meant an increase in military expenditures and destructive capability.

The promise of a SALT treaty in some cases has speeded up the rush toward more numerous and destructive weapons. Secretary of Defense Harold Brown, for example, recently directed Air Force and civilian analysts to accelerate planning for the best way to deploy the M-X missile so that President Carter could announce plans for the more deadly intercontinental missile in time to help ease the way for Senate approval of the SALT II agreement. SALT II will also allow the development of the Trident submarine, the longer-range Trident missile, the cruise missile, and the neutron weapons. The SALT II ceilings on missile launchers are not sacrificial ones. The United States has not wanted more launchers (as opposed to warheads) than it now has,

a level below the ceilings in SALT II. The Soviet Union
will have to dismantle approximately 150 to 250 aging
launchers, but it will more than compensate for these by
adding hundreds of warheads to its other missiles.

In brief, SALT II legitimizes the nuclear weapons below the ceilings, encourages building up to those ceilings,
and, outside the ceilings, explicitly allows new weapons that
will make future reductions more difficult. It fails to move
the United States, the Soviet Union, other nuclear powers,
and countries approaching nuclear capability closer to the
renunciation of nuclear arms.

Need Global Security System

Motivated by a desire to hold political ground against
the advance of growing conservative forces, many people
argue that advocates of arms reduction must work to ratify
a relatively useless SALT II primarily because we later on
want a more desirable SALT III. Yet this is an admission
that SALT II is not worth the lobbying effort in itself. If
that is so, we should lobby now for the comprehensive
arms reductions that we unrealistically hope will be part of
SALT III, and forget about SALT II. If such a lobbying
effort were successful, SALT II would be passed easily. In
other words, lobbying for a demilitarized global security
system would, as a side effect, encourage the ratification
of SALT II, but lobbying for SALT II will not give us
comprehensive arms reductions.

Organizations with offices in Washington get easily
caught up in counting votes to achieve legislative "victo-
ries," without careful assessment of whether a victory matters in the long run. A treaty ratification campaign offers a
concrete goal, something useful for mobilizing constituents
and contributors. It is exciting to have lunch with Washington influentials to plan strategy for a legislative battle.
Those tasks are important, but *only* when the battle is over
a fundamental issue, and SALT II definitely is not. None-

theless, during 1978, leaders from labor unions, liberal lobbying groups, and almost all peace organizations joined the SALT bandwagon.

Unfortunately, a campaign to ratify SALT II will lead the public into the mistaken belief that the best road to genuine arms reductions is through negotiations similar to SALT I and SALT II. Yet this approach will not produce a demilitarized security system because it aims to manage the arms competition, not to terminate it. Negotiators—no matter how well-intentioned—cannot reduce arms substantially at the same time that they rely heavily on them for security and diplomatic influence. Arms can be significantly reduced only when security can be achieved through means that do not depend so completely on national military forces. This requires us to think seriously not about piecemeal, stopgap measures of arms stabilization or control within the present international system, which is a war system based on the threat or use of force, but about steps to take toward the creation of an alternative security system.

A transnational monitoring agency that includes third parties is an essential part of any long-range policy to increase security while decreasing dependence on arms. Yet with characteristic arrogance the U.S. and Soviet governments act as if they were the only two governments in the world that have a right to monitor their nuclear postures—postures that cannot avoid affecting every inhabitant of the planet. Nor is it any credit to our NATO allies that they allow the United States to take this position. The verification of SALT II could be carried out by a global, multilateral agency. Establishing such an agency would be a positive accomplishment. Even with such an agency for monitoring SALT II, the United States could still maintain national means of verification to reassure those who might doubt the reliability of the global agency during its infancy. But because it has no long-range policy for arms reductions, and despite the absence of any reasonable argument against this idea, the United States refuses initiatives in this direction.

Promotes Great Power Dominance

Far from strengthening international peacekeeping organizations and increasing their representativeness, SALT II advances the system of great-power dominance over the economically and militarily less-powerful societies. The attitudes supporting SALT II will, in my opinion, someday be seen as a late-twentieth-century manifestation of old-fashioned imperialism. The Big Two, which produce ever-greater military fruits despite détente, hold most of the world's population hostage to the threat of instant genocide. Moreover, the world's people are subjected to taxation without representation—through the worldwide, negative economic consequences of unnecessary military expenditures. Much of the world's population suffers under political repression partly encouraged by militarism and alliance-building that are nurtured by U.S. and Soviet postures. The SALT II treaty may be a positive expression of political collaboration between the Kremlin and the White House, but it is not a serious effort to achieve a secure and peaceful world or a life of greater justice for many other societies of the world, conditions that are prerequisites to genuine peace.

Need Non-War System

To oppose the political Right is easier than to oppose the war system, but it is also less promising. To think seriously about abolishing war as an accepted institution means a fundamental questioning of the present international system, where we all enjoy privileges because of the present global distribution of power and wealth. Yet without commitment to demilitarization of the world security system, one or two weapons systems will come and go, as SALT fails or succeeds. But the return to new arms buildups, like the craving for a fix by an unreformed addict, will always return until steps are taken to kick the military habit completely—a message that should be carried to our Senators rather than the appeal to vote "yes" on SALT II.

For those who will work for ratification of SALT II, despite these arguments, I suggest that any Senator who is asked to vote "yes" on SALT also be asked to put meaning into that vote by a public pledge to vote for a 10 percent annual reduction in military expenditures, to be continued indefinitely if reciprocated by the Soviet Union. Of course, if a vote for SALT II were synonymous with a vote for a budget cut or even a freeze, the Pentagon would oppose it and SALT II would fail—unless a strong public movement had been established to insist on moving toward an alternative security system. This reality exposes the true meaning of SALT.

The nongovernmental arms-control community in 1979, supposedly on the cutting edge in pressing the government toward more enlightened policy, is actually far less progressive than were some government officials years ago. Since the 1950s, the growth of military influence and mentality in our Legislative and Executive chambers has spread to a majority of public-opinion leaders. That the spread has been without maliciousness does not make its impact upon the body politic any less malignant. In 1961, the U.S. representative to the United Nations could declare: "We do not hold the vision of a world without conflict. We do hold the vision of a world without war—and this inevitably requires an alternative system for coping with conflict. We cannot have one without the other." Today, such ideas are not even the object of serious study, let alone advocacy, by Washington arms controllers in or outside the government. Both the pro–SALT II Carter Administration and the anti–SALT II conservative Republicans accept most of the same assumptions about the international security system; neither group tries to change those assumptions. They say, in effect, "A war system is here to stay—at least during my term of office. To move beyond rhetorical flourishes and to take action to reverse the arms buildup and to replace the war system with a peace system is unrealistic."

Vietnam Parallel

The U.S. public and the world's public face a problem similar to the one we faced in the Vietnamese conflict. Few U.S. political leaders then wanted to suffer the assumed political costs to their own careers by advocating a withdrawal of U.S. personnel, regardless of how unpromising were the prospects for U.S. military forces. In the late 1970s, few political leaders are willing to accept the assumed political costs of advocating a practical program for abolition of war, regardless of how unpromising may seem the long-range prospects for continuing the escalation of armaments.

It is time for a new antiwar coalition to come together. In addition to familiar antiwar activists, this time it must include environmentalists, feminists who understand how deeply ingrained, erroneous, and unjust are the myths about power, the poor, who suffer the most from militaristic consumption of resources, and political conservatives who believe that some variation of a system of law and non-violent conflict resolution, which resolves disputes domestically, should be developed for world society.

Given the political will, it is possible to implement a feasible step-by-step approach that would move us toward the abolition of war as an accepted institution, much as slavery shifted in our thinking and behavior from an acceptable to an unacceptable human institution during the 1800s. In effect, the portion of human interactions across national boundaries that now is part of a war system would be transformed into a peace system. A peace system already governs many of those human interactions, such as trade and travel. The idea of abolishing war, which at first glance seems blushingly unrealistic, turns out upon further examination to be realistic enough that it already has been partly implemented. In fact, peaceful resolution of conflicts is the rule, not the exception, for most human inter-actions within nation-states and even in the majority of relations across national boundaries.

The full blossoming of the abolitionist idea depends upon cultivation by people bold and imaginative enough to see that nonviolent conflict resolution, with appropriate institutional reform and attitudinal change, can be ex-panded to all areas of international life.

Finally, unexamined enthusiasm for SALT comes easily because we have lost a clear moral sense of right and wrong. It is a tragic self-deception to think that the important point for peace advocates in 1979 is that we will be better off with SALT II than without it. A more accurate message is that the weapons that now exist and will remain after SALT II are morally unacceptable. No less than a gas chamber for innocents, a nuclear furnace for any purpose is a fundamental denial of the most revered ethical teach-ings of Western and non-Western civilizations.

Yet the U.S. and Soviet military postures are not aimed at eliminating the role of nuclear weapons or military power in human affairs—with or without SALT. The mili-tary officials of the two countries are not in alliance to spur the arms race and to violate the global human in-terest, but the effect is the same as if they were. And the mutual U.S.-Soviet military stimulation, with its attendant consequences of nuclear proliferation and destabilizing weaponry, poses a greater threat to the human race than does the present Soviet arsenal to the U.S. population.

WHY CHRISTIANS MUST REJECT SALT[3]

When I was invited to a briefing session for religious leaders at the State Department on October 18, 1978, I

[3] From article entitled "Is SALT Worth Supporting? No: Chaplains Bless-ing the Bombers," by Thomas J. Gumbleton, auxiliary bishop of Detroit and President of Pax Christi, U.S.A. *Commonweal.* 106:105–7. Mr. 2, '79. Copyright © 1979 Commonweal Publishing Co., Inc. Reprinted by permission.

went readily, because I had implicitly assumed I would support the signing of the SALT II Treaty. I was pleased to have an opportunity to learn more about the proposed treaty and to join with other religious leaders in the effort to build a base of support for SALT II in the churches and religious communities throughout the United States.

At the end of the morning session, after the facts had been carefully laid out about the incredibly large arsenals that the Soviets and the U.S. would have under SALT II, one of the participants asked a question. "Do you mean that you expect us as religious leaders to support the kind of arsenal you are describing? That we should offer religious legitimacy for weapons outlined in your presentation?"

The government representative who had just been speaking, indicated his awareness that support for such weapons might be troubling to a religious leader. But his response was that the Arms Control Agency and the State Department could not make moral evaluations. Their responsibility was to guarantee the "security" of the United States by making sure that even with a SALT II agreement, our arsenal would not be inferior to any nation's.

The impact of that response for me was immediate and challenging. The more I thought about it, the clearer the situation became. The government expert indicated that he and his colleagues would not deal with the kind of concern raised by the questioner. In fact, he was saying that that was a moral problem, a religious question—not a political one—and religious leaders had to be concerned with such questions. He understood that.

But who really was asking that kind of question? We had been brought together to be briefed and we were already devising a strategy to form a Religious Committee of Support for SALT II. We were going to help "sell" SALT II. The very religious leaders who should have been raising the challenging questions about the rightness of our arms policy were simply being "drafted" into an army of support for the treaty. Those in government were not going to ask such questions. And it seemed that those in positions of religious and moral leadership were not going to ask them either.

Raising the Moral Issue

But such questions must be raised. In my own reflection on the role of a religious leader and my responsibility to help people to face the moral implications of our government's decisions, I began to think again about that most fateful day in the history of the world: August 6, 1945. Hiroshima. One bomb exploded over that city and incinerated 80,000 to 100,000 people in 9 seconds—men, women, children.

I remembered Pope Paul VI in his Peace Day Statement of 1976, describing that bombing of Hiroshima as "a butchery of untold magnitude."

I began to ponder the fact that SALT II would legitimate the destructive power of 615,000 Hiroshima bombs, the present American arsenal.

I began to wonder how I as a religious leader could offer support for an agreement that would sanction that kind of destructive power in the hands of any government. I was especially troubled when I recalled that President Carter, within the last year in speaking before the United Nations, ruled out the use of nuclear weapons by the United States only against nations that do not themselves have such weapons. That statement left no doubt that we *do* intend to use them. And what is more, we intend to use them first.

On June 30, 1975, Defense Secretary James Schlesinger publicly stated: "Under no circumstances could we disavow the first use of nuclear weapons. . . . If one accepts the no first use doctrine, one is accepting a self-denying ordinance that weakens deterrence." That statement put the United

States clearly on public record as being ready and willing to be the first nation to use nuclear weapons in a confrontation with another nation. This policy has not been modified.

I remembered the pastoral letter of the American Bishops "To Live in Christ Jesus." This letter clearly states the moral position that Catholics are to be guided by regarding not only the use of weapons of indiscriminate destruction, but also concerning even the possession of such weapons:

> The right of legitimate defense is not a moral justification for unleashing every form of destruction. For example, acts of war deliberately directed against innocent non-combatants are gravely wrong, and no one may participate in such an act. . . .
>
> At the same time, no nation, our own included, may demand blind obedience. No member of the armed forces, above all no Christians who bear arms as "agents of security and freedom" can rightfully carry out orders or policies requiring direct force against non-combatants. . . .
>
> With respect to nuclear weapons, at least those with massive destructive capability, the first imperative is to prevent their use. As possessors of a vast nuclear arsenal, we must also be aware that not only is it wrong to attack civilian populations but it is also wrong to threaten to attack them as part of a strategy of deterrence. . . .

I was among the bishops who overwhelmingly voted approval of that statement. Am I now ready to repudiate that stance? Am I now ready instead to seek throughout the religious community support of a policy of our government that so recently has been clearly judged immoral?

The argument has been raised that at least SALT II puts a "cap" on the permissible number of such weapons. Yet as I thought about that, it seemed that supporting such an agreement would be like supporting a "cap" on the number of torture chambers permitted to governments. I can't accept that anyone who firmly believes that torture is immoral would be ready to support such a position. Torture is wrong, and we could never give our blessing to the maintenance of even one such facility.

"But can't you support SALT II as the first step in the right direction? Here we are, deeply inplicated in an immoral situation. We cannot extricate ourselves with one decisive action. It will take time, and we must do it one step at a time. SALT II is the first step in a journey of a thousand miles."

If only it were a first step. It is not.

Consider this report in the New York *Times* as recently as December 13, 1978:

George M. Seignious II, the Carter Administration's new director of the Arms Control and Disarmament Agency, told reporters today that even if Washington and Moscow succeeded in working out a new strategic arms accord soon, the United States would still have to press ahead with modernizing its nuclear arsenal.

While noting that he "wholeheartedly" supported the proposed arms agreement, he said that Moscow would be able under the accord to make improvements to its nuclear forces that would "doubtlessly propel" the Carter Administration into some form of military response. Business as usual under SALT II. The arms race goes on.

This is really the failure of SALT II. It is not the beginning of the reversal of the arms race. It is not the first step. The simple reason is that the arms race is no longer a matter of numbers. When our arsenal can already destroy every major Soviet city 36 times over, it is at least irrelevant, if not ridiculous and perhaps even deceptive to talk about a "cap" on numbers as though this begins the process of reversing the arms race.

At this point in the arms race it is a race in technology and sophistication. It is a race to increase the destructive capacity of the weapons we already possess. It is a race to increase the accuracy of these weapons. As noted in the New York *Times* (December 24, 1978), "In the view of many analysts, new arms agreements do not really limit arms competition, they only push it down different avenues."

SALT II will be no different in this regard from any past agreement. The Soviets, even with SALT II, will continue to plan five new land-based intercontinental ballistic missiles, a new strategic submarine and long-range bomber. And the same day that Secretary Vance went to Geneva to conclude the SALT II talks Zbigniew Brzezinski told reporters that the United States would soon have to embark on a multibillion dollar program for deploying mobile intercontinental missiles.

Clearly SALT II is not a first step out of an evil situation.

The Selling of SALT

Another clear reason why SALT II is not the first step in reversing the arms race is the kind of "selling job" that is being done for it. Instead of emphasizing that the arms race has brought us to the most dangerous point of insecurity for all nations that the world has ever known, our political leaders are still trying to convince us that we can have security and peace through nuclear arms. The arguments made for the treaty strongly emphasize that we are not lessening in any way our dependency on nuclear weapons. Einstein put it accurately when he said, "The unleashed power of the atom has changed everything but our modes of thinking, and thus we drift toward unparalleled catastrophe." A genuine first step in reversing the arms race would require some change in our thinking. Without that, a mere "cap" on numbers and even some slight limit on technology will be meaningless. We are still hostages with the nuclear gun pointed at our head.

It is very late in the history of the arms race. Very serious people indicate that nuclear war before the year 2000 is not just a possibility, it is a probability. Religious leaders, I think, have a major share of the responsibility for this situation. Before 1976 what pope or bishop referred to the bombing of Hiroshima as "a butchery of untold magnitude?" Until 1976—while the arms race had been going on for almost 30 years—where did we find clear moral guidance from Catholic bishops in the United States, or very many other religious leaders, similar to the statement in "To Live in Christ Jesus" quoted above? It has been pointed out in a National Council of Churches pamphlet that Karl Barth, who was a leader in the German churches' resistance to Hitler, once declared the most vital issue facing Christianity has been the inability of the churches to take a definite stand against nuclear weapons. He compared it to the churches' inability to take a stand against Hitler. By our failure in moral leadership we have acquiesced in that "drift toward unparalleled catastrophe" deplored by Einstein.

The call for us to support SALT II is "a moment of grace" when we must begin to give strong leadership and clear moral guidance. We must indicate to the President and to our people that we cannot in good conscience support SALT II.

There are some who will ask how can you align yourself with the opponents of SALT II who do not want any limitation on strategic arms whatsoever? The answer is simply that we are not in any way aligned with these opponents of SALT II. We do not agree with their understanding as to what will bring genuine security to our nation. Furthermore, I do not see any reason to engage in a debate with them over SALT II. We could win such a debate, but we would not have made any real progress toward reversing the arms race. I am convinced that a much better answer is simply to end formal negotiations and rely on unilateral demonstrations of arms restraint. Not only would this be in accord with our present moral teaching, but it would also be the most expedient thing to do—in the opinion of many specialists in and out of government.

If religious leaders and religious communities can be persuaded not to support SALT II, what can they offer instead in the effort to bring about genuine disarmament? I would suggest the following as an outline of a carefully conceived effort to reverse the arms race.

Reversing the Arms Race

First, the religious community should pledge itself to undertake a massive effort of education and conscience formation. We have a responsibility to begin to develop in ourselves and the whole community "a whole new attitude toward war," as Vatican Council II has called for. And we must really share the conviction of that same Council that "the arms race is an utterly treacherous trap . . . it is much to be feared that if this race persists, it will eventually spawn all the lethal ruin whose path it is now making ready." We must also share with others the moral judgment of the Vatican statement to the U.S. that "the arms race in itself is an act of aggression against the poor."

This is only the briefest sampling of the clear statements giving moral guidance on the arms race. Besides sharing these teachings we must pledge ourselves to seek out in prayer and faith what God has revealed to us, especially in Jesus, about the use of violence. Pope Paul in 1976, even appealed to us to consider as an example for our own time "what can be done by a weak man, Gandhi—armed only with the principle of non-violence." In 1978 Pope Paul urged us "to say 'no' to violence, and 'yes' to peace." We could prepare the way for the reversal of the arms race if we took very seriously our responsibility to teach and form consciences in the light of this ever more urgent teaching about non-violence.

The *second* step the religious community can take is to promote a national effort to build a climate for conversion from an arms industry to exclusively peace production. The churches could join in a community effort to prepare for such conversion of our industrial capacity by educating our people to understand the interrelationship between the arms race and unemployment, and many other social problems in the United States. And very concretely we could actively support the "Defense Economic Adjustment Act," a Senate bill (S2279 in the 95th Congress) intended to move us from an arms-based economy to one based on peacetime civilian-oriented priorities.

Thirdly, the religious community must take the lead in positively building peace. Vatican II stated: "Peace is not merely the absence of war. Nor can it be reduced solely to the maintenance of a balance of power between enemies. . . . Instead it is rightly and appropriately called 'an enterprise of justice' (Is. 32:7). Peace results from the harmony built into human society by its divine Founder, and actualized by men (and women) as they thirst after ever greater justice." (*Gaudium et Spes,* #78)

There is not the space here to go into detail on the program of justice we could develop, starting with changes in our own lifestyle and our use of this world's goods, but there surely is no lack of steps we could take in the struggle to assure that every person on earth begins to have enough to eat, decent shelter, adequate education and health care, and all the things necessary to meet basic human needs. Instead of forming a religious coalition of support for SALT II, we could form such a coalition to pass the world Peace Tax Fund Bill. This bill would provide an entirely new resource for peace programs. It could be the first step in assuring that our resources are used in the "enterprise of justice" rather than the continued escalation of the arms race.

In 1963 Pope John XXIII, a few weeks before his death, published his widely acclaimed letter, *Pacem in Terris.* In it he reminded us that "there is an immense task incumbent on all men (and women) of good will, namely, the task of restoring the relations of the human family in truth, in justice, in love and in freedom." (#163)

We must stop the arms race now and undertake this task with the greatest sense of urgency because the finish line in the arms race is not peace but holocaust.

A MAJOR DISAPPOINTMENT[4]

The prospective SALT II agreement, when considered in light of the fundamental objectives of the United States in both SALT I (November 1969 through May 1972) and, at the outset, SALT II, represents a major disappointment. It might be more modestly called "SALT 1.1."

The two basic objectives of the U.S. in the first round of Strategic Arms Limitation Talks were enhancing the stability of the strategic nuclear balance and constraining the costs of the arms competition. Stability, the principal objective, is a situation in which neither superpower sees an advantage in striking first in a crisis and neither feels compelled to undertake major new programs because of the perceived future danger of the other acquiring a first-strike advantage.

The anti-ballistic missile treaty of SALT I, by sharply limiting deployment and prohibiting some types of qualitative improvements, on balance served both U.S. objectives.

The SALT I Interim Agreement on strategic offensive arms, however, did not significantly advance U.S. objectives. That agreement (which expired in October 1977 but which both sides continue to observe) froze the level of strategic ballistic missile launchers. The Interim Agreement was soon overtaken by events, especially by major new Soviet ICBM programs, allowable as modernization under the agreement but which had surprising scope, momentum and capability. Prior to and during SALT I, there was only one Soviet ICBM program, the SS-9, which posed a potential threat to the survivability of the 1,000 U.S. silo-based Minuteman ICBMs. After SALT I, there are two: the SS-18

[4] Article entitled "What if SALT Breaks Down?" by Charles A. Sorrels, Senior Fellow in foreign policy studies at the Brookings Institution. *Wall Street Journal.* 141:14. Jl. 20, '78. Reprinted with permission of the *Wall Street Journal* © 1978 Dow Jones & Company, Inc. All Rights Reserved.

as successor to the SS-9, and the SS-19, a successor to part of the widely deployed SS-11 force.

For SALT II, the U.S. declared in 1972 that a principal objective would be to "constrain and reduce on a long-term basis threats to the survivability of our respective retaliatory forces."

In November 1974, an accord was reached at Vladivostok, meant to establish key provisions of a SALT II agreement to last through 1985. Both superpowers would accept an equal aggregate ceiling (including heavy bombers not included in the Interim Agreement) of 2,400 launchers, with a sublimit of 1,320 launchers with MIRVs (multiple independently targeted re-entry vehicles). Soviet acceptance of the principle of an equal aggregate ceiling—albeit high —may have been a fundamental accomplishment in SALT II.

However, it proved impossible during the Ford administration to translate the Vladivostok accord into a treaty because of disagreements both within the U.S. government and between the U.S. and the Soviet Union. The Soviet interpretation of Vladivostok was that U.S. long-range cruise missiles were included and constrained and the Soviet Backfire bomber was not. The U.S. position was that the long-range cruise missile was not covered by the accord and that the improving Backfire bomber, because it did have an intercontinental capability regardless of what priority mission the Soviets chose to assign to it, should be included in the formal SALT II agreement.

The Carter administration made an early attempt to break this deadlock. In March 1977, the U.S. proposed two basic options. The first would have implemented the U.S. interpretation of the Vladivostok accord and deferred "all issues relating to the cruise missile, Soviet Backfire bomber, and mobile ICBMs."

The second, "comprehensive" and preferred option would have substantially reduced (from 2,400 down to 1,800 to 2,000) overall levels of strategic delivery vehicles;

cut back modern heavy Soviet ICBMs (from 308 to 150);
prohibited new (such as mobile) types of ICBMs; limited
testing of ballistic missiles (e.g., to improve accuracy), and
limited cruise missiles' range to about 1,500 miles.

The Soviet leadership emphatically rejected both options.
Subsequent discussions agreed upon a three-part framework
for SALT II: a treaty through 1985 establishing overall
ceilings, a three-year protocol constraining deployment of
some new systems (such as cruise missiles and mobile
ICBMs) and a statement of principles relating to objectives for SALT III. The treaty would reduce by about 10%
the ceiling of 2,400 launchers set at Vladivostok and include that accord's subceiling of 1,320 MIRVed launchers.
The subceiling of 308 modern heavy Soviet ICBMs would
be continued from the Interim Agreement. A new sub-
ceiling of 820 MIRVed ICBMs, such as the SS-18 and SS-19,
would be so high (compared to 550 in the March proposal)
as to fail to constrain significantly the threat to Minuteman.

The U.S. appears to have moved toward the Russian
interpretation of Vladivostok. On the one hand, the United
States has agreed in the treaty to a range limitation on the
air-launched cruise missile and to counting bombers carrying them against the subceiling of MIRVed launchers. On
the other hand, the Backfire—which could reach a level of
nearly 400 by 1986—would not be counted in the aggregates
of the treaty but would instead be treated only in a separate
Soviet pledge of constraints on production rates and up-
grading.

By deciding not to count the Backfire directly in SALT,
the U.S. will have moved away from its commitment in
1973 not to "permit threats to our allies to develop un-
checked because of SALT agreements." Moreover, the administration has agreed to constraints in the protocol that
relate to ground- and sea-launched cruise missiles that
could be future "forward-based" systems (U.S. systems de-

ployed in countries such as Britain, capable of delivering nuclear weapons against Soviet territory).

Such inclusion in principle represents a fundamental change in U.S. policy from the outset of SALT I and II. The protocol would prohibit the deployment and restrict considerably the range of cruise missiles of high interest to NATO allies, particularly Germany and Great Britain. Thus, for the first time in SALT, the U.S. agreed to limiting medium-range systems that might be deployed in Europe.

In April 1977, in describing the comprehensive proposal, Secretary Brown stated that it would limit strategic uses of cruise missiles "but it would not make us pay for a SALT agreement by limits on our nonstrategic ability to counter Soviet weapons that are controlled neither in SALT nor elsewhere."

Uneasiness in Europe

Unfortunately, the subsequent course of the negotiations suggests to some Europeans that this is what has happened. They keenly believe that by allowing some limits on theater applications of cruise missiles in SALT II, the U.S. has "thrown away" a basis for bargaining for Russian restraint in its growing nuclear capability deployed against Europe (particularly the mobile, MIRVed SS-20, intermediate-range ballistic missile, the deployment of which has begun and is a matter of special concern to West Germany).

To reassure its NATO allies, the U.S. has argued that the protocol will only last for three years, will not interfere with development or realistic schedule of deployment, and is no precedent for the U.S. position in SALT III. European skepticism in response focuses on doubt that the Soviets would accept in SALT III less than they thought had been accomplished in SALT II.

The administration also stresses that within the period

of the protocol, which would also ban deployment of new types of ballistic missiles, the Soviets are well along in the development of yet another (fifth) generation of ICBMs and that their development pace would be constrained, while the U.S. development schedule for a mobile ICBM (MX) would not be curtailed.

SALT has not constrained some of the most important threats to the survivability and effectiveness of strategic forces, such as counterforce capability of ICBMs, air defenses in the Soviet Union, and antisubmarine warfare systems. Therefore, SALT cannot be expected to avoid the need for some substantial, expensive U.S. programs, such as development and deployment of a mobile MX system to reduce the vulnerability of and maintain the credibility of controlled response with the ICBM portion of the strategic triad.

Although token reductions of, say, 10% in the aggregate launcher levels may be characterized as beginning to "wind down the arms race," they are likely to have little budgetary impact.

On the other hand, given that the U.S. has hedged substantially against Soviet threats unconstrained by SALT, a breakdown in SALT would not necessarily require major new U.S. programs. The more immediate, important impact would be political, because although Soviet-American détente preceded SALT by several years, it is very doubtful that it would continue undamaged without SALT. However, basic Soviet and U.S. interest in avoiding high-risk political confrontations such as Berlin preceded SALT and those interests would remain despite the breakdown of negotiations or rejection of a SALT II treaty by the Senate.

The administration has estimated that without the SALT II aggregate ceiling of 2,400 (or 10% less), the Soviet Union could build up to "over 3,000" launchers by 1985. This is certainly possible. However, with the very high priority and heavy budgetary commitment of the Soviet Union to the continuing major momentum in strategic offensive programs, it is hard to visualize a much greater Soviet effort outside of SALT.

If the Soviets abandoned the ABM treaty in the aftermath of a failure of the SALT II process on strategic offensive arms, that would be a setback to a major accomplishment of SALT. However, the U.S. has already deployed MIRVs, one effective response to ABMs; and has developed more advanced re-entry systems for overcoming a new Soviet ABM system. Although there would be pressure to respond to a Soviet ABM deployment with a U.S. deployment, that "mirror image," expensive response would not be the only or best way to respond.

If the SALT II talks broke down, a principal objective of the U.S. would be to establish incentives for renewing them, combining demonstrated will to compete with an offer of restraint to be reciprocated. Although rhetoric about SALT frequently suggests that the alternative is an "arms race," the fact is that substantial competition has been continuing during SALT, with the U.S. becoming the more reactive party. Since the strategic balance is not self-regulating and SALT's realistic contribution to stability is only modest, carefully managed U.S. competitiveness—rather than being inherently antithetical to stability—is critically important to the difficult task of preserving stability.

IV. THE POST-SALT PROSPECTS

EDITOR'S INTRODUCTION

While Americans debate the virtues or defects of arms control as embodied in SALT II, the arms race itself whirls on—and is likely to continue doing so, whether SALT II is accepted or rejected. There appears to be no end to the ingenuity of scientists and military technologists in devising new ways for annihilating populations. The selections in this section emphasize the grim truth.

In the first article, Richard Pipes, a professor of history at Harvard, argues that the time has come for more realistic assumptions in our nuclear strategy, assumptions that are in line with the thinking of military planners in the Soviet Union. Speaking of the Soviet viewpoint on warfare, as seen in the voluminous literature available to Western analysts, Pipes writes, "SALT is hardly mentioned. The impression one gains from reading this material is that from the Soviet Union's vantage point, the purpose of arms limitation talks is not so much to reduce the nuclear arsenal as to restrain that particular aspect of U.S. power which it fears the most, namely advanced technology and the ability it gives us suddenly to neutralize the war machine which the Russians are building up so systematically and at such heavy cost."

The next article, from *Business Week,* warns Americans to expect nothing by way of reduced defense spending as a result of SALT II. On the contrary, both qualitative improvements and new innovations in our nuclear arsenal are expected to raise costs still further. The last article, by the director of the Stockholm International Peace Research Institute (SIPRI), though written in 1977, provides a review of the latest innovations in both the U.S. and Soviet Union and the increasing proliferation in what he calls "the mounting prospects of nuclear war."

TIME TO RETHINK NUCLEAR STRATEGY[1]

In the United States, there is a pronounced tendency, due perhaps to the high level of our technology and the positivist outlook which thrives in a technological environment, to regard man and society as conditioned by the tools they use.

It is, for instance, widely believed in this country that there exists such a thing as an "industrial society" with its particular system of values and code of behavior: this despite the fact that the record of history indicates quite convincingly that the introduction of advanced methods of mechanical production in one country (e.g. England) led to the reduction of the power of the state and contributed to liberalization, and in another (e.g. Germany) yielded the very opposite results.

It is not surprising, therefore, that the sudden appearance in 1945 of nuclear weapons should have been received in the U.S. in a manner consistent with the positivist outlook. American intellectuals assumed from the beginning that there inheres in these monstrous tools of destruction a logic obligatory on all who possess them.

That logic, in their view, rested on several related propositions: (1) that nuclear weapons were so destructive that they threatened not only the victim of aggression but all humanity, the aggressor included; (2) that no defense was possible against them; and (3) that, for both these reasons, they could have no conceivable political or military utility—except to deter others also armed with them.

These assumptions, still widely held today, underpin our approach to SALT and explain the critical importance which we attach to it both in our defense planning and in our relations with the Soviet Union.

[1] Article adapted from talk to Department of State entitled "Rethinking our Nuclear Strategy," by Richard Pipes, a professor of History at Harvard. *Wall Street Journal.* 141:26. O. 12, '78. Reprinted with permission of the *Wall Street Journal* © 1978 Dow Jones & Company, Inc. All rights reserved.

A cool, critical analysis of these assumptions, however, might well reveal that far from being axiomatic they are vulnerable on logical as well as pragmatic grounds. Let me point out a couple of glaring inconsistencies in our prevailing nuclear philosophy.

America's nuclear strategy rests on the concept of deterrence. But it ought to be quite clear that deterrence, whatever its merits, is anything but a strategy. Deterrence postulates that an adequate means of retaliation in the hands of one power will inhibit another power from launching a nuclear attack upon it. As such, it is a device for preventing war, not a guideline for the conduct of war.

Diplomacy vs. Military Strategy

Now the prevention of war is the province of diplomacy, not of military strategy: The latter normally takes over precisely at the point where the former fails and the parties to a dispute resort to arms. Of course, we have developed a variety of strategic options and targeting policies for the contingency of nuclear war. I doubt, however, whether we have a clear notion what these weapons are supposed to accomplish, should we be required to use them. Deeply imbedded in all our plans is the notion of punishing the aggressor rather than defeating him.

Secondly, consider the issue of nuclear supremacy. It is often argued, sometimes with the invocation of heaven's name, that the concept of nuclear supremacy is utterly meaningless because there is no way it can be exploited.

National security, it is said, requires nothing more (nor less) than strategic parity or "essential equivalence." One does not have to be an expert on formal logic to realize that the terms "parity" or "equivalence" postulate their contraries, which are "superiority" and "inferiority." He who says "parity" unavoidably admits to the possibility of "dis-parity," that is, superior and inferior entities. Were this not the case, we would have no need for arms limitations. We could readily permit the Russians to squander

their resources on accumulating until the end of time useless arsenals of still bigger and more accurate missiles while
we enjoyed the good life behind our deterrent.

As an insular nation, we have come instinctively to define strategic weapons to mean weapons capable of inflicting harm on one's homeland; and just as instinctively, we
have attributed this definition to the Russians. As a matter
of fact, however, except when it suits them for purposes of
negotiating certain arms limitations with us (as, for instance, in the case of the Backfire bomber), the Russians
have not adopted this definition at all.

Their criterion for determining what constitutes strategic weapons is not geographic but functional: A strategic
weapon to them is one which, regardless of its range, can
attain immediate strategic objectives, which always and
everywhere entail depriving the enemy of the capability
to offer resistance. The geographic criterion, that is, losses
of territory with the people and resources located on them,
has in their military thinking a secondary importance.

This attitude results in part from historic experience;
the Russians, who live in a country of open frontiers, have
learned over the centuries that the sacrifice of lives, territory
and resources is not, in itself, fatal, provided that the political authority and its military arm remain intact to
mount a counteroffensive at the appropriate moment. The
attitude also derives in part from intense thinking about
the science of war, of which the Russians are today, now
that the Germans have quit the field, the world's leading
addicts.

The arrival in the 1940s of nuclear weapons left the
leaders confused at first. In the mid-1950s they turned over
the problem of their military implications to high-level
committees.

We know little about the course of these committee discussions, but we do know that the decision reached by 1959
ran contrary to the prevailing U.S. view. Strategic weapons,
it was concluded, not only had their utility; they had be-

come the decisive instruments of modern warfare. The establishment in the winter of 1950–60 of the Soviet Strategic Rocket Forces as a separate service marked the onset of a fundamental transformation of Soviet military thinking and deployment that is still in the course of implementation.

In the interwar years, the German Reichswehr had developed a novel strategy for rapid breakthroughs of static defenses centered on the tank which the British had invented in World War I. Similarly, the Russians had taken over the U.S.-developed nuclear warhead, fitted it onto the German-devised rocket, and formulated a fresh strategy in which, in violation of all the canons of traditional warfare, strategic objectives are to be secured in advance of tactical operations.

I believe that we are as oblivious to these staggering innovations in the art of war as the French and the British in their time had been to the German strategy of the armored Blitzkrieg. There is a striking parallel between their faith in passive defenses anchored on the Maginot Line and ours in a "sufficient" deterrent.

Soviet forces are structured around nuclear weapons and their tactics adapted to them. Russian generals do not deny the possibility of conventional engagements between the major powers, but they look upon these as mere skirmishes in a protracted conflict in which the employment of strategic weapons will prove crucial. It will be crucial because the punishment which the enemy's nuclear missiles can inflict on one's armed forces—the troops, their command and their logistic support—is potentially so devastating that no commander can consider deploying them for combat until and unless this threat has been substantially lifted.

This, of course, entails preemption, and its literature leaves no doubt that the Soviet Union intends massively to preempt the instant the leaders have arrived at the conclusion that war is unavoidable. In other words, the decision to resort to strategic nuclear weapons is not one likely to confront them on its own merits; rather, it will follow from the decision to wage general war.

Nuclear Preparedness Will Decide

I do not wish to be misunderstood. I am not saying that the Soviet High Command is plotting a surprise nuclear attack on the United States or its allies. The Soviet leaders are undoubtedly well aware of the risks and consequences of nuclear war. What I am saying is that they regard a general war to be possible, and have concluded that in such a war nuclear weapons will decide the issue. This being the case, they draw the further inference that the side that has prepared itself most thoroughly for fighting a nuclear war, both offensively and defensively, stands a better chance to emerge intact from it.

It is the task of Soviet diplomacy to avert war; it is the task of the Soviet military to win it, speedily and with the least losses, should diplomacy fail. It is difficult to fault this chain of reasoning.

These various considerations help explain why SALT plays so insignificant a role in Soviet strategic thinking. In the voluminous Soviet literature on modern warfare, SALT is hardly mentioned. The impression one gains from reading this material is that from the Soviet Union's vantage point, the purpose of arms limitation talks is not so much to reduce the nuclear arsenal as to restrain that particular aspect of U.S. power which it fears the most, namely advanced technology and the ability it gives us suddenly to neutralize the war machine which the Russians are building up so systematically and at such heavy cost.

We ought to make certain that just as they seek to circumvent our strategy by deterring our deterrent, we circumvent theirs. This can best be accomplished by subjecting ourselves in SALT to the least restraints on technology.

I will not presume to offer a military strategy to meet the Soviet threat. This is not something that professors of history ought to attempt—nor, for that matter, professors of government, economics or physics; nor retired diplomats. This surely is the legitimate province of the professional military, who are charged with the responsibility for implementing the nation's strategic plans should war break out.

However, before such a strategy can be formulated, it is essential to take a serious look at the premises underlying our strategic posture as well as those of our most formidable potential enemy, free of the presumption that just because we happen to have been the first with nuclear weapons, we have a unique insight into their nature and uses.

LOOK FOR RISE IN DEFENSE COSTS[2]

Assuming ratification by the Senate late this year [1979] the Strategic Arms Limitation Treaty (SALT II) . . . will have a paradoxical impact on future U.S. defense budgets. Despite the treaty's restrictions on development and deployment of both nations' strategic weapons, U.S. spending on strategic arms will not drop. Rather, it will rise sharply through 1985, the year SALT II is due to expire.

From 1975 through 1980 such spending will have totaled $53 billion. Over the next five years, assuming a 9% annual inflation rate, this price tag may grow an additional 50% or more.

"We have no choice," says one White House official, "but to modernize our strategic forces and take steps to protect them" against the nuclear arsenal—especially the 308 SS-18 heavy intercontinental ballistic missiles (ICBMs), each with 10 warheads—that SALT II will still permit the Soviets to deploy in silos.

U.S. spending on strategic weapons would rise even more dramatically, however, should SALT II fall through and the Soviets run wild with numbers of new missiles and

[2] Article entitled "SALT II's Paradox: Higher Defense Costs." *Business Week*. p 47–8. My. 28, '79. Reprinted from *Business Week* by special permission. Copyright © 1979 by McGraw-Hill, Inc.

warheads. Defense Secretary Harold Brown estimates, for example, that, lacking a treaty, the U.S. in the next decade might have to spend $30 billion more than it now contemplates to keep pace with the Soviet Union. Other officials think Brown's projection is much too conservative.

But such budget projections are unlikely to wash on Capitol Hill. Senate liberals and moderates alike already are asking why the treaty presages an increase, not a cut, of U.S. strategic-weapons spending.

The Higher Costs

Consequently, the Administration is in the predicament of having to justify the increase while selling SALT II to the Senate as a brake on the nuclear arms race. Brown fears the treaty "will create a sense of euphoria" and evoke sentiment in Congress "against modernizing and strengthening" U.S. strategic weapons.

There are several reasons why the U.S. will have to upgrade such weapons. The main one is that the increasing accuracy and power of Soviet ICBMs—chiefly the SS-18s—will have made the entire U.S. arsenal of 1,054 land-based ICBMs vulnerable to attack, in their fixed silos, by 1983. Thus, the U.S. plans to spend up to $40 billion to replace much of this arsenal with 200 new, more powerful ICBMs that it will disperse in aircraft, tunnels, or among several thousand additional silos to keep the Soviets from targeting them exactly. In justifying this plan, Brown declares: "SALT II did not cause our problem of missile vulnerability, and it will not cure it."

By cutting the number—but increasing the lethality—of such ICBMs, the U.S. would be left free, within SALT II limitations on total numbers of ballistic missile launchers, to deploy many more than the 13 General Dynamics Corp. Trident ballistic-missile submarines—each costing $1.5 billion—it had planned. This will mean many more missiles with which to arm them.

Such a production increase also is in store for the air-launched cruise missiles, at $1.5 million apiece, that Boeing Co. and General Dynamics have begun to turn out at a slow rate this year. SALT II permits 28 such missiles aboard an aircraft, each of which is counted among the total number of "heavy" or intercontinental bombers that the treaty limits. This means, says an Administration source, that "we have tremendous flexibility to pursue a very large cruise missile program," to the tune of about $6 billion.

It also means the U.S. must go through with a $2.5 billion program to modernize the B-52 bombers that will carry either—but not both—cruise missiles or nuclear bombs. William J. Perry, Defense Under Secretary for research and engineering, says the aging B-52s will be structurally sound until the 1990s. "But their avionics are outdated and are getting too expensive to maintain, so we are undertaking major replacements."

Meanwhile, the Air Force is busily designing a new bomber that "doesn't have swing wings but otherwise looks remarkably like the B-1" that Carter stopped from going into production two years ago, according to one Administration source. To carry cruise missiles, the service is also considering short-takeoff-and-landing (STOL) transports that Boeing and McDonnell Douglas Corp. have developed. In the end such aircraft could be "the really big sleeper costs" in future Defense Department budgets, says one official.

DRIFTING TOWARD ARMAGEDDON[3]

The probability of a nuclear world war is steadily increasing. If just the consequences of recent advances in military technology and the worldwide spread of this tech-

[3] Article entitled "The Mounting Prospects of Nuclear War," by Frank Barnaby, director of the Stockholm International Peace Research Institute (SIPRI). *Bulletin of the Atomic Scientists.* 33:10–20. Je. '77. Reprinted by permission of the Bulletin of Atomic Scientists, a magazine of science and public affairs. Copyright © 1977 by the Educational Foundation for Nuclear Science, Chicago, IL.

nology are considered, this conclusion is virtually inescapable. But there are other reasons for this pessimistic conclusion. Some of the main ones are:

—the arms race is now leading to a first-strike capability by both the United States and the Soviet Union,

—the growth of peaceful nuclear technology is spreading the capability of producing nuclear weapons all over the globe,

—the international trade in arms is rapidly militarizing the entire globe,

—and, finally, the current arms control approaches have failed. They have failed to restrain the nuclear arms race; they have failed to prevent the proliferation of nuclear explosives, and they have failed to control the arms trade—let alone lead to nuclear disarmament.

Given the catastrophic nature of a nuclear world war, this increasing probability of its occurrence is, to say the least, alarming.

Quantitatively, both the United States and the Soviet Union have enormous strategic nuclear arsenals. The United States admits to having 2,124 strategic nuclear delivery systems: 1,054 land-based intercontinental ballistic missiles (ICBMs) ; 656 submarine-launched ballistic missiles (SLBMs), on 41 strategic nuclear submarines; and 414 strategic bombers. The U.S. arsenal can deliver about 8,500 independently targetable nuclear warheads.

The Soviet Union is thought to have 2,404 strategic nuclear delivery systems: 1,452 ICBMs; 812 SLBMs on 60 strategic nuclear submarines, and about 140 strategic bombers. The Soviet arsenal can deliver about 4,000 independently targetable nuclear warheads.

And, in addition to their 12,000 or more strategic nuclear warheads, the United States and the Soviet Union have tens of thousands of tactical nuclear weapons in their arsenals, mostly much more powerful than the atomic bomb that destroyed Hiroshima.

But, as awesome as these numbers are, recent *qualitative*

developments in offensive and defensive strategic weapons and delivery systems are as dangerous, if not more so, than the size of these nuclear arsenals.

Both the United States and the Soviet Union are improving their strategic nuclear forces qualitatively along roughly the same lines. The United States remains ahead of the Soviet Union in almost all areas of strategic nuclear technology, but the gap is closing. Much more information is available about U.S. weapons than about Soviet ones, and so a description of developments inevitably, but unfortunately, emphasizes U.S. systems.

Warhead Delivery

The most dangerous current development in strategic nuclear weapons is the continuous improvement of the accuracy of warhead delivery. This accuracy is normally measured by the circular error probability (CEP)—the radius of a circle, centered on the target, within which 50 percent of the warheads aimed at the target will fall.

The current U.S. Minuteman III ICBM multiple independently targetable re-entry vehicle (MIRV), for example, probably has a CEP of about 350 meters (1,148 feet) at a range of 13,000 kilometers (8,078 miles). But the guidance system of the Minuteman III—the NS 20—is capable of providing a CEP of about 200 meters (666 feet). And the new MIRV under development for Minuteman III—the Mark 12A—is expected to have this accuracy. The Mark 12A will be capable of destroying enemy missiles in hardened silos.

Recently deployed Soviet ICBMs—the SS-17 (with four MIRVs), the SS-18 mod. 1, and the SS-19 (with six MIRVs) —are thought to have CEPs of about 600 meters (1,968 feet), a considerable improvement on earlier Soviet ICBMs.

The next generation of U.S. guidance systems—currently planned for the MX ICBM, the proposed replacement for the Minuteman III—is expected to provide CEPs of about 100 meters (328 feet). And in the generation after that, warheads will presumably be guided right on to their targets; CEPs as small as 30 meters (98 feet) will probably be achieved. These warheads, likely to be available in the mid-1980s, may also be provided with a maneuvering capability so that they can take evasive action against missile defenses. Such maneuvering independently targetable re-entry vehicles (called MIRVs) will represent the ultimate in accurate ICBM delivery systems.

Military technology has virtually attained the theoretical maximum also in warhead design. The Minuteman III MIRV, for example, weighs only about 100 kilograms (220 pounds) and yet has an explosive power equivalent to that of 200,000 tons (200 kilotons) of TNT. The Hiroshima bomb weighed four tons, had an explosive power of 12 kilotons, and was delivered by a B-29 bomber, a delivery system with an extremely large CEP.

These extraordinary developments in military technology since World War II show that the only significant limits on military research and development—the activity which makes the arms race possible—have been the innovative capabilities of the Soviet and American peoples. There is no reason why this rate of progress should not be sustained—in fact, it will probably continue to increase. Where then will military technology take us in the next 30 years?

The Spread of Nuclear Weapons

At the end of 1976, the world's nuclear power reactors had a total generating capacity of about 79,000 megawatts of electricity (MWe). This nuclear capacity, provided by 173 power reactors in 19 countries, was capable of producing 16,000 kilograms of plutonium annually. About 30 percent of it was in 15 non-nuclear weapon countries: Argentina, Belgium, Bulgaria, Canada, Czechoslovakia, the Federal Republic of Germany, the German Democratic Republic, India, Italy, Japan, the Netherlands, Pakistan, Spain, Sweden, and Switzerland.

By the end of 1980, about 250,000 kilograms of plutonium will probably have been accumulated worldwide. Austria, Brazil, Finland, Hungary, Iran, South Korea, Taiwan and Yugoslavia will also then have nuclear power reactors. And by 1984, 28 non-nuclear weapon countries will probably have nuclear power reactors with a potential annual plutonium production rate of about 30,000 kilograms—theoretically enough to produce 10, 20-kiloton atomic bombs per day.

The major problem in controlling the spread of nuclear weapons is that the fissile material for atomic bombs can be produced on a relatively small scale. A 40-megawatt electrical graphite-moderated, natural-uranium reactor could, for example, produce about 20 kilograms of plutonium-239 per year, more than enough for two 20-kiloton atomic bombs. The components for such a small reactor could be easily and secretly obtained on the open market for a cost of less than $20 million. The reactor and a small chemical reprocessing unit to remove the plutonium from the reactor fuel elements could be clandestinely constructed and run.

Many countries have deposits of uranium ore within their borders and so it would normally not be difficult to obtain fuel for such a reactor. The small reactor route may well be the one chosen even by countries with large peaceful nuclear power programs, if they should decide to produce atomic bombs.

This does not, of course, mean that the possibility of the diversion of plutonium from a peaceful nuclear power program to military purposes should be ignored. Nor does it necessarily mean that the current concern over the acquisition of nuclear power reactors, reprocessing plants or enrichment plants by new countries is misplaced. But, contrary to public opinion and often even to official statements, it does mean that a lack of access to a commercial reprocessing plant need not (and probably would not) prevent the proliferation of nuclear weapons to countries which make the decision to acquire them.

The problem of controlling plutonium will be even

more difficult if, and when, breeder reactors are developed to a commercial stage. The elements from the breeder blanket—in which uranium-238 is converted into plutonium—will normally contain plutonium with a 95 to 98 percent plutonium-239 content, excellent material for the manufacture of atomic bombs.

The plutonium in the spent fuel elements from the core of a breeder reactor will normally contain about 70 percent plutonium-239, which is about the same concentration as the plutonium in the spent fuel elements from a typical non-breeder reactor. This "contaminated" plutonium would still be usable as the fissile material for atomic bombs, albeit of less than optimum efficiency.

The military uses of highly enriched uranium (over 40 percent uranium-235) include the use of this material for the trigger of a hydrogen (thermonuclear) bomb, and, with plutonium, for the manufacture of more efficient atomic bombs. The spread of uranium-enrichment plants could, therefore, contribute to the proliferation of nuclear weapons. Once again, attention has been mainly focused on plants large enough for commercial use. But a small enrichment facility—a dozen or so centrifuges, for example—would be enough to produce the kilogram-per-year quantities of suitably enriched uranium needed for the development of a modest nuclear weapon force. The relatively high degree of enrichment necessary could be obtained by repeatedly recycling the uranium through the system.

Non-Proliferation Efforts

The major suppliers of nuclear material and equipment have, for the past few years, periodically held secret meetings in London to discuss ways of making the nuclear market place less anarchic. The aim is to minimize the risk of the diversion of nuclear technology—a technology which they are so eager to supply—to the production of nuclear explosives. The very fact that these meetings are deemed necessary is essentially an official admission of the failure of the Non-Proliferation Treaty (NPT) to establish a viable non-proliferation régime.

Countries that are party to the NPT are committed to have International Atomic Energy Agency (IAEA) safeguards applied to *all* their nuclear facilities, whether indigenously constructed or imported. A sensible course of action to slow down proliferation would be for the exporters to insist that their clients accede to the NPT, or at least subscribe to the same system of international safeguards as that which the parties to the NPT are required to take on. So far the suppliers have failed to establish such a rule.

It is unrealistic to hope that any new international measure to establish a non-proliferation régime will succeed where the NPT has failed. The most that can be hoped for is that measures will be taken to slow down the rate of proliferation. Such measures include a moratorium on the construction of reprocessing plants and breeder reactors until the necessity for these reactors is unambiguously demonstrated, and multinational uranium-enrichment plants are under IAEA safeguards.

But the most essential action of all is the demonstration by political leaders of the nuclear-weapon states that they see no political or military value in nuclear weapons. This they could most convincingly do by undertaking nuclear disarmament.

A new nuclear-weapon power should be able to produce a 20-kiloton atomic bomb with a weight of about 1,000 kilograms, even at an early stage in its nuclear-weapon program. Such a warhead could be transported by many delivery systems, some of which are already in the arsenals of many near-nuclear countries, including the American A-4 Skyhawk, the F-104 Starfighter and the F-4 Phantom; the French Mirage V; the British Canberra and Buccaneer, and the Soviet Ilyushin 28.

Surface-to-surface missiles such as America's Honest John, Lance, Pershing and Sergeant; the Soviet Scud and Frog, and Israel's Jericho are all nuclear-capable. Moreover the technology of a peaceful space program could produce, as by-products, guided missiles suitable for short-, medium- and long-range ballistic delivery systems for nuclear warheads.

Recent developments in cruise missile technology could have far-reaching consequences for the proliferation of credible nuclear delivery systems—both tactical and strategic. Apart from their relative invulnerability, modern cruise missiles have two important characteristics: they are very accurate and relatively cheap. Many states, underdeveloped as well as developed, may see cruise missiles as highly desirable tactical and strategic delivery systems.

Most countries, including underdeveloped ones with a moderately sized defense industry producing, say, jet aircraft and missiles, could produce effective (even though relatively unsophisticated) tactical cruise missiles should they choose to do so. Many of these countries would, or will soon be able to, produce cruise missiles suitable for use by them as credible strategic delivery systems. Such non-industrialized countries with well-developed defense industries include Argentina, Brazil, China, India, Israel and Taiwan. If present trends continue, this list will quickly grow.

International Commerce

The major exporters of nuclear material and equipment are the United States, the Soviet Union, the United Kingdom, Canada, France, the Federal Republic of Germany, Sweden and Japan. In many of these countries, however, the nuclear exporters are private companies.

—*Canada* has exported two nuclear power reactors, one to India and one to Pakistan; and is constructing a power reactor in Argentina, India, and South Korea.

—The *Federal Republic of Germany* has constructed a power reactor in Argentina and in the Netherlands; and is constructing one in Austria, two in Brazil, two in Iran, one in Spain, and one in Switzerland.

—*France* has contructed a power reactor in Belgium and in Spain; and is contructing another one in Belgium.

—The *United Kingdom* has constructed one power reactor in Italy and one in Japan.

—The *United States* has constructed 26 power reactors abroad: Belgium (3), the Federal Republic of Germany (2), India (2), Italy (2), Japan (6), the Netherlands (1), Spain (2), Sweden (1), Switzerland (3) and the United Kingdom (4). Currently, the United States is constructing 26 more power reactors abroad: Brazil (1), Italy (1), Japan (4), South Korea (2), Mexico (2), Spain (7), Sweden (2), Switzerland (2), Taiwan (4) and Yugoslavia (1).

—The *Soviet Union* has exported five power reactors: Bulgaria (2), and the German Democratic Republic (3). It is now constructing 14 power reactors abroad: Czechoslovakia (4), Finland (2), the German Democratic Republic (6) and Hungary (2).

—*Sweden,* the only other exporter of nuclear power reactors is constructing two in Finland.

The 92 nuclear power reactors constructed or being constructed abroad by the major nuclear exporters have a total electrical generating capacity of 46,000 megawatts electrical. But international cooperation in nuclear energy extends far beyond the construction of these power reactors. Uranium enrichment plants, reprocessing plants and other key elements of the nuclear fuel cycle are involved.

Bilateral agreements, in fact, cover virtually all conceivable types of nuclear assistance and involve many countries. In some cases, both parties to bilateral nuclear agreements are underdeveloped countries. India has nuclear agreements with Afghanistan, Argentina, Bangladesh, Egypt, Iraq, and the Philippines. Argentina has agreements with five other Latin American states and with Libya.

International governmental nuclear transactions form a complex web of agreements. In addition, some transactions are not formalized in government agreements and some may be secret. And then there are the purely commercial transactions.

The nuclear industry has become a multibillion dollar concern, with cutthroat competition. The stakes are so high that nuclear issues are often decided on the basis of narrow commercial and national interests instead of the consequences for nuclear-weapon proliferation.

Dangers Posed by Nuclear Accidents

As there are many thousands of nuclear weapons in the world's arsenals, a significant portion of which are on alert, it is hardly surprising that nuclear weapon accidents occur. But few realize just how frequently they do occur. The data on nuclear-weapon-system accidents given in the *SIPRI Yearbook 1977* suggests that there have been at least 125 such accidents in the past 30 years—a frequency of one every three months.

Thirty-two accidents are listed, involving American weapon systems, in which nuclear weapons were believed to have been destroyed or seriously damaged. In 59 other American accidents, nuclear weapons may have been in danger of destruction or serious damage. Also listed are 22 Soviet nuclear weapon incidents, eight British, and four French. And the lists, relying as they do on open sources, are certainly incomplete.

Some of these accidents are bizarre. A U.S. Corporal missile with a nuclear warhead is recorded as "rolling off a truck into the Tennessee River." On April 9, 1968 the U.S. strategic nuclear submarine, *Robert E. Lee,* "became snagged in the nets of a French trawler" in the Irish Sea.

Among the Soviet incidents is one in which "American personnel recovered a nuclear weapon from a Russian airplane that crashed in the Sea of Japan." And in September of 1974 a Soviet guided-missile destroyer allegedly exploded and sank in the Black Sea. A number of Soviet nuclear-powered submarines have been snagged by Norwegian or

Japanese fishing boats. Some have collided with American submarines.

On at least nine occasions U.S. submarines, some of them armed with nuclear weapons, have collided with other, apparently Soviet, vessels within or close to Soviet territorial waters while on intelligence-gathering missions. There are probably similar incidents involving Soviet nuclear-armed submarines on intelligence missions. Such events vividly recall President Kennedy's warning of the danger of a nuclear world war being started by an accident.

World Military Spending

SIPRI estimates show that total world military expenditure in 1976 was about $334 billion, a 3,000 percent increase since 1900 (in constant prices). If the U.S. intelligence estimate of the dollar-cost (U.S.) of 1976 Soviet military activities ($130 billion) is used instead of SIPRI's estimate ($61 billion), then total world military expenditure in 1976 exceeds $400 billion.

The SIPRI figure is calculated from the Soviet national budget converted to U.S. dollars using SIPRI estimates of the rouble/dollar purchasing power parity. The SIPRI calculation takes into account the fact that the cost of some military activities—such as military R&D, military aid and stockpiling, and the military elements of the nuclear energy program—are considered not to be fully covered by the Soviet budget. The U.S. intelligence figure is a calculation of how much it would cost in the United States to develop, procure, maintain and operate a military force like that of the Soviet Union.

According to SIPRI figures, the major alliances—NATO and the Warsaw Treaty Organization—spent about 70 percent of the total world military expenditure. The Third World (excluding China) spent $51 billion, or 15 percent of the total. The Middle East spent about 53 percent of total Third World (excluding China) military expenditure; the Far East (excluding China) and Africa (excluding

Egypt) spent 13 percent each; South America spent 11 percent; South Asia spent 8 percent; and Central America, 2 percent. China has given no budgetary data since 1960, but a rough estimate of its military expenditure indicates that in 1976 it spent about 10 percent of total world military expenditure.

The military expenditures of individual Third World countries vary considerably. In 1975, for example, the three top spenders out of 93 Third World countries were Iran, Egypt, and Saudi Arabia, which spent (in current prices) $7.3 billion, $5.4 and $4.4 billion, respectively. These three countries accounted for 36 percent of Third World military expenditure. Israel spent $3.6 billion; and India, $2.6 billion. These five countries together accounted for 49 percent of Third World expenditure.

Each of another seven countries (Nigeria, Iraq, Brazil, Argentina, Libya, South Africa and Indonesia) spent between $1 and $2 billion. These top twelve countries—five of them in the Middle East—together accounted for 70 percent of Third World military expenditure.

An impression of the burden that military spending can become is given by the fact that Israel's 1975 gross domestic product per capita (in current dollars) was about $3,600 out of which about $1,050 was spent on the military; for Egypt the figures are $302 and $140, respectively. In comparison, the U.S. per capita military expenditure (the highest of all developed countries) in 1975 was about $425.

SIPRI's valuations of international deals in major weapons (tanks, ships, missiles and aircraft) are based on the annual arms trade registers it constructs and a list of comparable constant prices for the different types of major weapons supplied. The SIPRI figures do not, therefore, show the actual monetary value of major-weapon transactions. Most of these transactions in any case involve credit arrangements of some kind and others are on a grant basis. The SIPRI figures are designed to provide an index of the amount of resources involved in the arms trade.

Major weapons probably account for about one-half of the total trade in weapons and equipment. The remaining items traded include spare parts, small arms, ammunition, and support equipment.

The four biggest arms-producers—the United States, the Soviet Union, the United Kingdom, and France—continue to dominate the trade in major weapons. In the 1970s, these four countries supplied about 90 percent of the major weapons sold. The United States supplied 39 percent of the major weapons sold to the Third World; the Soviet Union supplied 33 percent, and the United Kingdom and France each supplied 9 percent.

During the 1970s, the Middle East was the largest regional importer of major weapons in the Third World, accounting for about 52 percent of the major weapons imported, followed by the Far East (including Vietnam) with about 15 percent.

According to SIPRI valuation, the value of major weapon deliveries to the Third World in 1976 was more than 16 percent higher than that in 1975. This increase was due mainly to large deliveries of U.S. weapons to Iran, Israel, Saudi Arabia and South Korea. About 40 percent of U.S. exports of major weapons in 1976 went to Iran, and about 12 percent went to each of the other three. The United States accounted for about 50 percent of total exports of major weapons to the Third World in 1976, the Soviet Union accounted for about 20 percent and the United Kingdom and France for about 8 percent each.

If there were no international trade in arms, participants in arms races—at least qualitative ones—would be limited to a few industrialized countries able to support sufficient military R&D activities to develop new weapons. But as it is, arms races are almost worldwide. In 1976, a total of 95 countries imported major weapons—tanks, ships, missiles or aircraft. About 105 countries, 75 of them in the Third World, imported military equipment of some type.

An increasing number of Third World countries produce weapons, or their components, under licensing arrangements with industrialized countries. Participation in co-production projects with foreign companies, although relatively rare at present, is also increasing. Argentina, Brazil, Colombia, Egypt, India, Indonesia, North Korea, South Korea, Pakistan, Peru, the Philippines, Singapore, Taiwan, and Venezuela all produce major weapons, or parts of them, under licenses issued by China, Czechoslovakia, France, the Federal Republic of Germany, Israel, Italy, Spain, Switzerland, the United Kingdom, the United States, and the Soviet Union.

Military Uses of Space

Publicity about satellites, and about space activities in general, normally focuses on their peaceful applications. Consequently, there is little public debate about the military use of space, in spite of the fact that about 60 percent of U.S. and Soviet satellites are military ones. Since the space age began, 1,386 military satellites are known to have been launched: 551 by the United States, 817 by the Soviet Union, 5 by the United Kingdom, 8 by France, 2 by China, and 3 by NATO.

Satellites for miltary communications, over both short and long distances, satellites for weather prediction, and satellites for accurate navigation are among the types used by the military. But perhaps the most important types are satellites used for photographic and electronic reconnaissance, to identify all sorts of military targets; satellites to position military targets accurately; satellites used to give early warning of the launching of enemy missiles; and satellites capable of intercepting and destroying orbiting enemy satellites.

Up to the end of 1976 the United States had spent about $30 billion on its military space activities, about one-third of the total sum spent on space. The cost of the Soviet military space program is kept secret, but the magnitude of the effort is similar to that of the United States.

China, France, the United Kingdom, and NATO also operate military satellites. The exact purpose of the Chinese satellites is not known, but photographic reconnaissance is probably included. In fact, two of them (those launched on November 26, 1975 and December 7, 1976) ejected recoverable capsules. French, British, and NATO military satellites have so far been only for communication, meteorologic, and geodetic purposes.

In 1976 the United States launched 4 photographic reconnaissance satellites whereas the Soviet Union launched 34. Many of these satellites had on board high-resolution cameras for "close-look" missions. The U.S. Big Bird satellite, launched on July 8, 1976, orbited for 158 days, a much longer lifetime than that of any Soviet photographic reconnaissance satellite. It is because of the relatively long lifetimes of its newer satellites that the United States can perform its space reconnaissance missions with such a small number of satellites.

Other military satellites launched in 1976 by the United States included 1 for electronic reconnaissance, 1 for navigation, 11 for communications, 1 for geodetic purposes, 4 for ocean surveillance, 3 for weather forecasting, and 1 early warning satellite. In 1976, the Soviet Union launched 9 electronic reconnaissance satellites, 8 navigation satellites, 29 communication satellites, 1 geodetic satellite, 2 ocean surveillance satellites, 5 weather satellites, 1 early warning satellite, and 7 intercepter-destructor satellites. The only other miltiary satellite launched in 1976 was a NATO communications satellite.

Considerable efforts are currently being made to increase the survivability in war of military satellites. Research into, for example, protection of orbiting satellites against nuclear attack from a hostile satellite is actively underway. Also under investigation are detection systems for early warning of satellite attacks, based on the surveillance of space by ground- and space-based sensors.

In the long-term, the most revolutionary military technological development may turn out to be the use of navigational and geodetic satellites to guide missiles on to their target. There is no reason why CEPs of a few meters over intercontinental ranges should not be obtained by these means. Moreover, the space-based navigation system of one country may be used by others for military purposes. This, coupled with the almost inevitable proliferation of, for example, cruise missile technology, is an extremely worrisome prospect.

The other side of the coin is the useful role of satellites in verifying, by "national technical means," some arms control agreements.

Arms Control Efforts

There was virtually no progress in 1976 in efforts to slow down the Soviet-American arms race and to limit armaments. . . . The 1974 Threshold Test Ban Treaty, and the 1976 treaty governing peaceful nuclear explosions remained unratified. Since a threshold ban may indefinitely delay a comprehensive ban on nuclear tests it may be better for disarmament if these treaties are never ratified.

The Vienna talks on the mutual reduction of forces in Central Europe were almost at a standstill. The two sides merely agreed that reductions should be carried out by stages: that U.S. and Soviet troop strengths would be dealt with apart from those of the other nine states; and that tanks, nuclear warheads, aircraft and other nuclear weapon delivery vehicles could be among the weapons to be reduced. But there was still disagreement about the extent of the reductions and how they should be implemented.

At the end of 1976, the UN General Assembly decided that a convention on environmental warfare should be opened for signature. The convention prohibits military or any other hostile use of environmental modification techniques having "widespread, long-lasting or severe" effects as the means of destruction, damage or injury to another state party.

The convention may be taken to legitimize modification techniques such as rain-making, the effects of which are other than "widespread, long-lasting or severe." Perhaps more seriously, the convention does not deal with such environmental damaging military operations as the use of herbicides and strategic bombing.

All in all, the convention is valueless even as an arms-control measure and is certainly not a step toward disarmament. During 1976, negotiations about urgently needed measures, particularly a comprehensive nuclear test ban and a prohibition of chemical weapons, remained in the doldrums.

During 1976, 40 nuclear explosions were announced or are presumed to have been conducted: 15 by the United States, 16 by the Soviet Union, 4 by France, 1 by the United Kingdom, and 4 by China. One of the Soviet explosions was probably for peaceful purposes. The rest were almost certainly nuclear weapon tests. These nuclear explosions bring the total number between 1945 and the end of 1976 up to 1,081: 614 by the United States, 354 by the Soviet Union, 64 by France, 27 by the United Kingdom, 21 by China, and 1 by India. The numbers themselves dramatically demonstrate the need for a comprehensive nuclear test ban.

Chemical Warfare Agents

The tragic accident that occurred in Seveso, Italy, on July 10, 1976, demonstrated again the potential of dioxin (2,3,7,8-tetrachlorodibenzo-p-dioxin) as a chemical-warfare agent. Dioxin is one of the most poisonous substances synthesized. It is easy to produce; it maintains its integrity very well, and can be easily disseminated. These characteristics make dioxin a highly suitable agent for a number of hostile military purposes.

The dissemination of dioxin, as a contaminant of "agent orange," during the Vietnam war was the first significant contamination of man's environment with dioxin. Estimates indicate that a total of more than 110 kilograms of dioxin was spread, mainly during a four-year period, over about a million hectares of South Vietnam's inhabited forest and farmlands. In the Seveso incident, about 2.5 kilograms is estimated to have spread in a matter of hours over about 230 hectares of inhabited farmland.

From the available evidence it is quite clear that dioxin is rapidly incorporated into an ecosystem and taken up by the living things within it. Once present it is almost impossible to remove. A conceivable military use for dioxin would be as an area-denial weapon. The consequences of such use would be to make the contaminated area uninhabitable for a very long period of time. Wildlife would be virtually eliminated and a major ecological imbalance produced. Seveso is our most recent reminder of the urgent need for a comprehensive prohibition of the development, production and stockpiling of chemical weapons.

In modern war, munitions, particularly missiles and major weapons, are likely to be used at a very high rate. During the 18-day October 1973 Arab-Israeli War, for example, about 600 aircraft, 3,000 tanks and 16 ships were lost at an average rate of one aircraft about every 40 minutes, one tank every 9 minutes and one ship every 27 hours. The immediate financial cost of the war has been estimated at about $20 million per hour. Because of the international arms trade the military forces of even small powers come to rely on the most up-to-date armament.

The main recipients of arms can become bound to their suppliers, almost as strongly as if they were allies. In particular, the knowledge that victory in war may well depend upon the receipt of lavish supplies of munitions throughout the fighting can result in the great-power supplier becoming the virtual guarantor of the survival of the client state. The rate of loss of weapons and the consumption of munitions was so high during the October 1973 war that both sides requested additional supplies from their great-power suppliers within a very few days of the outbreak of the fighting.

In a future conflict, a war in an unstable region involving such client states may escalate to a general nuclear war between the two great powers. The conflict may start as a conventional war but escalate to a local nuclear war fought with the nuclear weapons of the regional powers. This nuclear war could then escalate further to the involvement of the great powers, intent on preventing the annihilation of their clients. This chain of events is most likely if it starts at a time when one of the great powers perceives the chance of making a first-strike. In fact, the pressures for escalation may, under such circumstances, be so strong that only a very strong-willed political leader could resist them.

Some argue that the bonds formed between states as a result of bilateral and multilateral cooperation in economic, social and political affairs are sufficiently strong, or may soon become so, to overcome tendencies toward such a confrontation. But given the speed at which military technology is advancing and spreading throughout the world, and the frailty and uneven progress of international détente, it is reasonable to doubt this argument. Those that do, and those who are not prepared to rely on the hope that sufficiently responsible political leaders will be in power in the right countries at the crucial times to avoid a nuclear world war, have an obvious option—to work for nuclear disarmament.

To say that nuclear disarmament is impossible in today's world is not only incorrect but may be tantamount to saying that nuclear war is inevitable.

BIBLIOGRAPHY

An asterisk (*) preceding a reference indicates that the article or part of it has been reprinted in this book.

BOOKS, PAMPHLETS, AND DOCUMENTS

Abrahamsson, Bengt. Military professionalization and political power. Sage Pub. '72.

Alexander, Arthur J. Decision-making in Soviet weapons procurement. Adelphi paper, no. 147–8. International Institute for Strategic Studies (London) . '78.

Atlantic Council. Nuclear power and nuclear weapons proliferation. 2 vols. '78. (Westview Pr., Dist.)

Bader, William B. United States and the spread of nuclear weapons. Pegasus. '68.

Barnaby, Charles F. and Ronald Huisken. Arms uncontrolled. Stockholm International Peace Research Institute. Harvard University Pr. '75.

Barnet, Richard J., The economy of death. Atheneum. '69.

Bechhoefer, Bernard G. Postwar negotiations for arms control. Brookings Inst. '61.

Benoit, Emile. Defense and economic growth in developing countries. Lexington Books. '73.

Blechman, Barry M. and others. The Soviet military buildup and U.S. defense spending. (Studies in Defense Policy.) Brookings Inst. '77.

Bletz, Donald F. Role of the military professional in United States foreign policy. Praeger. '72.

Buchan, Alastair F., ed. A world of nuclear powers? American Assembly. Prentice-Hall. '66.

Burt, Richard. Reducing strategic arms at SALT: how difficult, how important? From Future of arms control. Part I: beyond SALT II. International Institute for Strategic Studies. '78.

Clayton, James L. The economic impact of the cold war: sources and readings. Harcourt, Brace. '70.

Colton, Timothy J. Commissars, commanders, and civilian authority: the structure of Soviet military politics. Harvard University Pr. '79.

*Costello, Mary. Politics of strategic arms negotiations. Editorial Research Reports, My. 13. '77.

DePorte, A. W. Europe between the superpowers: the enduring balance. Yale University Pr. '79.

Dinerstein, Herbert S. Soviet foreign policy since the Cuban missile crisis. Johns Hopkins Pr. '76.

Enthoven, Alain and K. W. Smith. How much is enough? Shaping the defense program, 1961–1969, Harper and Row. '71.

Epstein, William. Last chance: nuclear proliferation and arms control. Free Pr. '76.

Farley, Philip J. and others. Arms across the sea. Brookings Inst. '78.

Frank, Lewis Allen. Soviet nuclear planning: a point of view. American Enterprise Institute for Public Policy Research. '77.

Gati, Charles, ed. Caging the bear: containment and the cold war. Bobbs-Merrill. '74.

Gati, Charles and Toby Trister Gati, The debate over détente. Headline Series 234. Foreign Policy Assoc. F. '77.

Goldman, Marshall. Détente and dollars: doing business with the Soviets. Basic Books. '75.

Goldsborough, James O. NATO—past and future. Headline Series 244. Foreign Policy Assoc. Ap. '79.

Gompert, David C. and others. Nuclear weapons and world politics: alternatives for the future. Council on Foreign Relations. McGraw-Hill. '77.

Hackett, Sir John (General) and others. The Third World War: August 1985. Macmillan. '79.

Hamer, Joh. World arms sales. Editorial Research Reports. Vol. 1. No. 17. My. 7, '76.

Harkavy, Robert E., The arms trade and international systems. Ballinger Pub. '75.

Imai, Ryukichi. Nuclear safeguards. Adelphi papers, no. 86, International Institute for Strategic Studies. Mr. '72.

International Institute for Strategic Studies. The military balance, 1976–77. Westview Pr. '76.

International Institute for Strategic Studies. The military balance, 1978–79. Westview Pr. '78.

Jonsson, Christer. Soviet bargaining behavior: the nuclear test ban case. Columbia University Pr. '78.

Kahan, Jerome H. Security in the nuclear age: developing U.S. strategic arms policy. Brookings Inst. '75.

Kalb, Marvin and Bernard Kalb. Kissinger. Little, Brown. '74.

Karp, Walter. The politics of war. Harper. '79.

Kennedy, Gavin. The military in the Third World. Scribner. '75.

Klare, Michael T. War without end: American planning for the next Vietnams. Vintage Books. '72.

Lefever, Ernest W. Nuclear arms in the third world: U.S. policy dilemma. Brookings Inst. '79.

Luttwak, Edward N. Strategic power: military capabilities and political utility. Center for Strategic and International Studies. Sage Pub. '76.

Maddox, John. Prospects for nuclear proliferation. Adelphi papers, no. 113. International Institute for Strategic Studies. Spr. '75.

Marks, Anne W., ed. NPT: paradoxes and problems. Arms Control Assoc. '75.

Marwah, Onkar and Ann Sculz, eds. Nuclear proliferation and the near-nuclear countries. Ballinger Pub. '75.

Neal, Fred Warner, ed. Détente or debacle: common sense in U.S.-Soviet relations. American Committee on East-West Accord. Norton. '79.

Newhouse, John. Cold dawn: the story of SALT. Holt, Rinehart & Winston. '73.

Paul, Roland A. American military commitments abroad. Rutgers University Pr. '73.

Pierre, Andrew J., Nuclear politics: the British experience with an independent strategic force, 1939–1970. Oxford University Pr. '72.

Pierre, Andrew J. with Claudia W. Moyne. Nuclear proliferation: a strategy for control. Headline Series 232. Foreign Policy Assoc. O. '76.

Quanbeck, Alton H. and Barry M. Blechman. Strategic forces: issues for the mid-seventies. Brookings Inst. '73.

Quester, George H. The politics of nuclear proliferation. Johns Hopkins Pr. '73.

Ra'anan, Uri and others, eds. Arms transfers to the third world: the military buildup in less industrial countries. Westview Pr. '78.

Rhinelander, John B. and Mason Willrich. SALT: The Moscow agreements and beyond. Free Pr. '75.

Rosen, Steven, ed. Testing the theory of the military-industrial complex. Lexington Books. '73.

Russett, Bruce M. What price vigilance? The burdens of national defense. Yale University Pr. '70.

Schilling, Warner R. and others. American arms and a changing Europe: dilemmas of deterrence and disarmament. Columbia University Pr. '73.

Sharp, Admiral U. S. G. Strategy for defeat. Presidio Pr. '78.

Sivachev, Nikolai V. and Nikolai N. Yakovlev. Russia and the United States: U.S.-Soviet relations from the Soviet point of view. University of Chicago Pr. '79.

Sivard, Ruth Leger. World military and social expenditures, 1976. WMSE Publications, Box 1003, Leesburg, VA. 22075.

Slocombe, Walter and others. Controlling strategic nuclear weapons. Headline Series 226. Foreign Policy Assoc. Je. '75.

Stanton, John and Maurice Pearton. The international trade in arms. Praeger. '72.

Stoessinger, John G. Henry Kissinger: the anguish of power. Norton. '76.

Stockholm International Peace Research Institute (SIPRI). Arms control: A survey and appraisal of multilateral agreements. Taylor & Francis Ltd. (London). '78.

Stockholm International Peace Research Institute (SIPRI). The nuclear age. Almqvist & Wiksell (Stockholm). '74.

Stockholm International Peace Research Institute (SIPRI). Resources devoted to military research and development. Amqvist and Wiksell (Stockholm). '72.

Stockholm International Peace Research Institute (SIPRI). SIPRI Yearbook '79. Taylor & Francis Ltd. (London). '79.

Talbott, Strobe. Endgame: the inside story of SALT II. Harper and Row. '79.

Udis, Bernard. From guns to butter: technology, organizations and reduced military spending in Western Europe. Ballinger Pub. '78.

Udis, Bernard, ed. The economic consequences of reduced military spending. Lexington Books. '73.

Ulam, Adam B. The rivals: America and Russia since World War II. Viking Pr. '71.

UNA-USA National Policy Panel. Controlling the conventional arms race. United Nations Association of the USA. N. '76.

United Nations. Department of Economic and Social Affairs. Disarmament and development. UN. '73.

*United Nations. Department of Political and Security Council Affairs. Economic and social consequences of the arms race and of military expenditures. Updated report of the Secretary-General. UN. '78.

United States Arms Control and Disarmament Agency. World military expenditures and arms trade 1963–1973. Washington, D.C. '75.

United States Congressional Budget Office. Assessing the NATO/Warsaw Pact military balance. Washington, D.C. USGPO. D. '77.

United States Senate, Committee on Government Operations. Nuclear proliferation and the International Atomic Energy Agency. Library of Congress. Mr. '76.

Van Cleave, W. R. and S. T. Cohen. Tactical nuclear weapons: An examination of the issues. Crane, Russak. '78.

Weidenbaum, Murray. The economics of peacetime defense. Praeger. '74.

Weiler, Lawrence D., ed. The arms race: secret negotiations and the Congress. Stanford University Pr. '76.

Willrich, Mason and Theodore B. Taylor. Nuclear theft: risks and safeguards. Ballinger Pub. '74.

Wohlstetter, Albert and others. Nuclear policies: fuel without the bomb. Ballinger Pub. '78.

Wolpin, Miles D. Military aid and counterrevolution in the Third World. Lexington Books. '72.

PERIODICALS

America. 140:124, 127–30. F. 24 '79. SALT II: the arms race to end all arms races; with editorial comment. J. J. Fahey.

Aviation Week and Space Technology. 110:22–3. F. 12, '79. Basing concepts could violate SALT. A. K. Marsh

Aviation Week and Space Technology. 110:22. F. 26, '79. Carter praises emerging SALT terms.

Aviation Week and Space Technology. 110:14–16. Ap. 16, '79. Soviets push telemetry bypass. C. A. Robinson Jr.

Aviation Week and Space Technology. 110:11. Ap. 23, '79. Defense Crisis. Robert Hotz.

Aviation Week and Space Technology. 110:29. Ap. 30, '79. Carter details SALT verification views: excerpts from remarks. Ap. '79. Jimmy Carter.

Aviation Week and Space Technology. 110:30. Ap. 30, '79. Iranian monitor loss minimized.

Aviation Week and Space Technology. 110:30. Ap. 30, '79. Soviet arms control ruled by military.

Aviation Week and Space Technology. 110:20. My. 7, '79. Carter avers arms treaty can be verified.

Aviation Week and Space Technology. 110:9. My. 14, '79. With or without SALT; excerpts from address. Samuel Nunn.

Aviation Week and Space Technology. 110:14–16. My. 14, '79. SALT 2 approval hinges on MX. C. A. Robinson Jr.

Aviation Week and Space Technology. 110:14–16. My. 21, '79. Acceptable basing mode for MX sought. C. A. Robinson Jr.

Aviation Week and Space Technology. 110:17–18. My. 21, '79. NATO members urge SALT 3 parleys. Eugene Kozicharow.

*Bulletin of the Atomic Scientists. 33:10–20. Je. '77. The mounting prospects of nuclear war. Frank Barnaby.

Bulletin of the Atomic Scientists. 35:15–21. Ja. '79. In defense of SALT. Michael Mandelbaum.

Bulletin of the Atomic Scientists. 35:4. F. '79. High price of SALT. B. T. Feld.

Bulletin of the Atomic Scientists. 35:63–4. F. '79. Salty debate in the Senate. D. N. Schwartz.

Bulletin of the Atomic Scientists. 35:81. Mr. '79. Great arms race. D'Arcy Richardson.

Bulletin of the Atomic Scientists. 35:6–7. Ap. '79. Preview: the Soviet experts and SALT. W. C. Matthias.

Bulletin of the Atomic Scientists. 35:10–14. Ap. '79. Policy assessment at the crossroads: the Soviets and SALT. W. D. Jackson.

Bulletin of the Atomic Scientists. 35:11–14. My. '79. European security: three proposals: Mutual and balanced force reductions negotiations. David Linebaugh.

Bulletin of the Atomic Scientists. 35:7–9. My. '79. Good and bad of nuclear arms control negotiations. G. B. Kistiakowsky.

*Business Week. p 47–8. My. 28, '79. SALT II's paradox: higher defense costs.

Business Week. p 62–4. Je. 4, '79. Carter customizes his pitch to unions.

Christian Century. 96:172–4. F. 21, '79. SALT II and the survival of liberty. Michael Novak.

Christian Century. 96:343–7. Mr. 28, '79. Challenge of SALT II. H. E. Fey.

*Commentary. 67:23–32. F. '79. Case against SALT II. E. V. Rostow.

*Commonweal. 106:105–7. Mr. 2, '79. Is SALT worth supporting? No. Thomas Gumbleton.

*Commonweal. 106:108–10. Mr. 2, '79. Is SALT worth supporting? Yes. J. B. Hehir.

Commonweal. 106:168–70. Mr. 30, '79. Next war. Thomas Powers.

*Department of State Bulletin. 78:17–23. O. '78 SALT Two—the home stretch. Address by Paul C. Warnke.

Department of State Bulletin. 79:5–7. F. '79. Interview of December 19; transcript of program; 1978 interview by Walter Cronkite. Jimmy Carter.

Department of State Bulletin. 79:14–15. Ap. '79. Preserving freedom and peace in a nuclear age; address, February 22, 1979. W. F. Mondale.

*Department of State Bulletin. 79:24–7. Je. '79. The facts of SALT II. Leslie H. Gelb.

Foreign Affairs. 54:207–32. Ja. '76. Assuring strategic stability in an era of détente. Paul Nitze.

Foreign Affairs. 54:763–87. Jl. '76. Market-sharing approach to the world nuclear sales problem. Abraham Ribicoff.

Foreign Affairs. 57:492–502. F. '79. High hopes and hard reality; arms control in 1978. McGeorge Bundy.

*Foreign Affairs. 57:245–68. Winter '78–9. SALT II and American security. Jan M. Lodal.

Foreign Policy. 18:30–43. Spr. '75. The high price of nuclear arms monopoly. Alva Myrdal.

Fortune. 96:176–9+. O. '77. What to hope for, and worry about in SALT. F. C. Iklé.

*Harpers. 258:21–9. My. '79. Arms bazaar; SALT was never intended to disarm. Robert C. Johansen.

Journal of Conflict Resolution. 18:502–13. S. '74. Economic assessment of the military burden in the Middle East: 1960–1980. Fred Gottheil.

Journal of Social and Political Affairs. p 107–46. Summer '78. The nuclear warfighting dimension of the Soviet threat to Europe. Amoretta Hoeber.

Macleans. 92:36. My. 21, '79. SALT II: a long way from over: verification issue. William Lowther.

*Nation. 226:622–6. My. 27, '78. Thirty years of escalation. Sidney Lens.

Nation. 228:453. Ap. 28, '79. Movable missiles; multiple aimpoint system and SALT II.

Nation. 228:587. My. 26, '79. Kissinger's dream.

National Review. 31:290–4+. Mr. 2, '79. SALT II primer: Interview with Henry Kissinger. H. A. Kissinger.

National Review. 31:342+. Mr. 16, '79. Destabilizing the world; J. Carter's speech at Georgia Tech.

National Review. 31:502–3. Ap. 13, '79. Movement on SALT. W. F. Buckley Jr.

National Review. 31:523–4. Ap. 27, '79. No SALT.

National Review. 31:612+. My. 11, '79. Fire one on SALT; views of Paul Nitze. J. A. Rehyansky.

National Review. 31:597–8. My. 11, '79. SALT: tune in to next week's exciting chapter.

National Review. 31:698–9. My. 25, '79. Let us reason together. W. F. Buckley Jr.

New Republic. 180:3. F. 17; 180:3. My. 19, '79. TRB from Washington.

New Republic. 180:9–11. Ap. 21, '79. Treaty push II. John Osborne.

*New Republic. 180:5–6+. My. 5, '79. We support SALT.

New Republic. 180:14–16. My. 26, '79. Improved odds. Morton Kondracke.

Newsweek. 93:32–3. F. 19, '79. Hard SALT sell. Peter Goldman and others.

Newsweek. 93:46+. Ap. 23, '79. Key SALT issue; verification issue. David Butler.

Newsweek. 93:108. Ap. 23, '79. Unthinkable? Meg Greenfield.

Newsweek. 93:28–9. Ap. 30, '79. SALT skirmishing. David Butler and others.

Newsweek. 93:116. My. 7, '79. War games. Meg Greenfield.

Newsweek. 93:65. My. 14, '79. Moscow's helping hand. Fred Coleman.

Newsweek. 93:65–6. My. 14, '79. SALT delays. Fay Willey and others.

Newsweek. 93:36–40. My. 21, '79. SALT II: and now for the battle. David Butler and others.

Newsweek. 93:43–4. My. 21, '79. Two views on SALT; excerpts from interviews by J. J. Lindsay. Paul Nitze; Paul Warnke.

Newsweek. 93:104. My. 28, '79. How to think about SALT. G. F. Will.

Newsweek. 93:50. My. 28, '79. Soviets on SALT. Georgii Arbatov.

Newsweek. 93:46–7. S. 24, '79. SALT II on the rocks. David Butler and others.

New York Review of Books. 26:33–8. Mr. 22, '79. False alarm: the story behind SALT II. G. B. Kistiakowsky.

New York Times. p 1+. Ag. 9, '79. Pro-arms coalition formed in Congress. Richard Burt.

New York Times. p 1 and 18. S. 9, '79. President opposes tying Cuba dispute to arms pact vote. Bernard Gwertzman.

New York Times. p A15. S. 13, '79. Cuba issue may delay a vote on Soviet Arms Pact. Charles Mohr.

New York Times. p A22. S. 13, '79. Senate military bloc warms to new Carter Arms Pact. Steven Roberts.

New York Times. p 21. S. 22, '79. Reject SALT, but seek genuine nuclear disarmament. William Westmoreland.

Progressive. 43:8. Mr. '79. Sanguine about SALT.

Progressive. 43:5–6. My. '79. SALT moratorium. Sidney Lens.

Readers Digest. 114:97–102. My. '79. Fateful illusions of SALT II. R. K. Bennett.

Time. 113:17. Ja. 29, '79. On trusting the Soviets: views of Paul Warnke. Hugh Sidey.

Time. 113:34+. Ap. 16, '79. Twin salvos for SALT.

Time. 113:20–21. Ap. 23, '79. Some pepper for SALT; J. Glenn's verification criticism.

Time. 113:21. Ap. 30, '79. If Moscow cheats at SALT; verification issue.

Time. 113:22. Ap. 30, '79. It began with a cigarette. Hugh Sidey.

Time. 113:21. My. 7, '79. SALT II: the long vigil.

Time. 113:12–13. My. 14, '79. Atmosphere of urgency.

Time. 113:22–3. My. 21, '79. Special report: Now the great debate.

Time. 113:25–6+. My. 21, '79. Special report: Who conceded what to whom; how Carter and Co. negotiated the strategic arms treaty. Strobe Talbott.

Time. 113:36+. My. 21, '79. Special report: To educate their senators.

U.S. News & World Report. 86:35–6. Ap. 2, '79. Selling SALT: President pulls out the stops.

U.S. News & World Report. 86:92. Ap. 16, '79. SALT: the Senate's role. Marvin Stone.

U.S. News & World Report. 86:23. Ap. 30, '79. Pot starts boiling.

U.S. News & World Report. 86:21–7. My. 21, '79. SALT II: special report.

U.S. News & World Report. 86:38–9. My. 28, '79. As battle for SALT shapes up in Senate—.

Vital Speeches of the Day. 45:322–5. Mr. 15, '79. New perspectives on our relations with China and the Soviet Union; address, February 1, 1979. W. V. Roth Jr.

Vital Speeches of the Day. 45:397–402. Ap. 15, '79. Limitations of armaments and arms control; address. February 17, 1979. S. R. Resor.

Vital Speeches of the Day. 45:450–3. My. 15, '79. SALT II address, April 25, 1979. Jimmy Carter.

*Wall Street Journal. 141:14. Jl. 20, '78. What if SALT breaks down? Charles Sorrels.

*Wall Street Journal. 141:26. O. 12, '78. Rethinking our nuclear strategy. Richard Pipes.

Wall Street Journal. 143:1+. Mr. 22, '79. In the SALT debate, Sen. Sam Nunn's role could prove decisive. Albert Hunt.

*Wall Street Journal. 143:26. Je. 21, '79. An earlier attempt to limit arms. C. H. Fairbanks Jr.

Wall Street Journal. 144:20. Jl. 25, '79. Linking politics to SALT. Stephen Sestanovich.

Washington Monthly. 11:26–31. My. '79. Why Warnke quit. N. Lemann.

Washington Post. p A6. Ag. 25, '78. Missile 'Shell Game' is consistent with SALT, Warnke says. Don Oberdorfer.

Washington Post. p A3. O. 31, '78. Arms curb protocol praised by Warnke. George Wilson.

Washington Post. p A23. N. 3, '78. SALT's emotional core. Stephen Rosenfeld.